# Reflections on Certain Qualitative and Phenomenological Psychological Methods

Amedeo Giorgi, PhD

University Professors Press
Colorado Springs, CO
www.universityprofessorspress.com

First Published in 2018, University Professors Press.

ISBN 13: 978-1-939686-25-1

University Professors Press
Colorado Springs, CO
www.universityprofessorspress.com

Front Cover Art by Richard Bargdill
Cover Design by Laura Ross

In his latest book, Giorgi confronts several current traditions in qualitative research including grounded theory, hermeneutics, descriptive phenomenology, and heuristic research, and offers critical discussion of their underlying philosophical positions, as well as the possibility for engaging in human science research drawing from more than one position. His clarifying distinctions between various uses of interpretation, including its more limited application within his own descriptive phenomenological method, advances our understanding of an old controversy within phenomenological psychology: where does *description* stop, and at what point do researchers find themselves engaging in one or another form of *interpretation*? More importantly, Giorgi offers incisive definitions of what constitutes description as well as what constitutes the psychological attitude that underlies it.

Beyond his definitions and comparisons, Giorgi also offers one of his best demonstrations of the method in a return to his earlier research on learning, this time bringing out the meaning of Husserl's *noetico-noematic* method in his analysis of learning. The volume concludes with a critique of the recent trend toward "naturalizing" phenomenology, reaffirming that phenomenology is not only non-naturalistic, but anti-naturalistic.

A solid, sustained analysis and clarification of where we stand today in some of the qualitative methods that have helped to shape psychology's advance in its own methodological self-understanding.

Scott Churchill, PhD
Editor, *The Humanistic Psychologist*
Professor, University of Dallas


Giorgi drills deeper and more detailed into the salient issues of scientific phenomenological research. He provides a collegial critique of others' works that is inspired by phenomenology, but shows in this volume how his approach is founded upon it. Giorgi's over 50-years of contributions to human science research are further clarified in this collection of essays. Anyone embarking on a phenomenological approach in his or her research would be better prepared by studying this book.

Rodger Broomé, PhD
Assistant Professor, Utah Valley University

Over a half century ago, Amedeo Giorgi was a pioneer in establishing a human 'scientific' alternative to psychology's reliance on the methodologies of the physical sciences. Before Giorgi, while critiques of psychology's reductionism were plenty, these same critics too often defaulted to the selfsame methods that accompanied the actual materialistic approaches they were critiquing. Psychologists were restricted to the methodological straitjacket of an empiricism that forced meanings into experimental measurables. A truly 'human' psychology could not be fully realized without a methodology in keeping with what is unique to the human domain: meaning-making and subjectivity itself. Giorgi changed all of this by developing a simple, yet step by step, systematically descriptive procedure for studying the inherently psychological dimension of lived experience and meaning. What was not simple was the systematic theoretical underpinnings he gave to this methodology through the application of phenomenological epistemology to this new approach to psychological research. Any qualitative methodology that does not escape the metaphysics and epistemology of empiricism will perpetually work against itself. To this end, Giorgi takes up Husserl's theory of intuition as the correct and necessary epistemological foundation to a truly psychological psychology.

While a plethora of new qualitative methodologies have mushroomed since the 90s (some deriving from Giorgi's own work), few of these methods affirm the phenomenological theory of science that grounds Giorgi's approach. One could say that the current standing of qualitative psychology is one that is dominated by the ubiquitous relativistic dogma that "everything is an interpretation." While the anti-science trend of postmodernism and the relativism of constructivism have long departed the fields of philosophy and the other humanities, this lingering influence on qualitative research in psychology maintains a pervasive hold. In due time, as these trends necessarily dissipate, qualitative psychologists may soon rediscover in Giorgi what was always there at the very birth of qualitative psychology—a time-tested rigorous methodology grounded in a phenomenological philosophy of science.

These essays reveal Giorgi in his prime as he surveys the current field of qualitative psychology. Drawing on a rich 60-year career as one of psychology's most distinguished theoretical psychologists, we see Giorgi take up the issues crucial to the possibility of a truly qualitative psychology. Non-phenomenological as well as pseudo-phenomenological methods are critically distinguished and evaluated with discernment and care. We see in these important essays an unrelenting passion for the possibility of a psychology fitting to its name—a science of the human spirit.

James Morley, PhD.
Professor of Clinical Psychology
Ramapo College of New Jersey

# Table of Contents

# Chapter 1

## Three Different Qualitative Methods and the Philosophies That Support Them

In recent years, the use of qualitative methods for research in psychology has become increasingly acceptable. There are today a diversity of methods from which researchers can choose (see Denzin and Lincoln, 2000; Wertz et al., 2011). The choice of a method to use is usually left to the researcher, who rarely has to justify the method selection as long as the method is an already established one. Perhaps it is too early to make an assessment of the relative merits of the existing qualitative methods, but one important way to discriminate among the existing methods is by becoming aware of the philosophies behind them. Today, there are already too many methods to cover adequately in an article. However, there are at least three distinct philosophies being utilized, and it might be important to highlight the relative values embedded in each of these philosophies.

Clearly, the philosophy that supports most of the methods is some type of empiricism. This is because empiricism is the oldest philosophy of science in the West, and indeed for many years the only philosophy supporting scientific work, especially for the natural sciences. However, since the beginning of the twentieth century, two other philosophies have emerged that have found applications in psychology: phenomenology and hermeneutics. In this article, I want to indicate the guiding role that each philosophy plays with respect to the scientific method that has evolved from it. Since it is more familiar, I shall begin with an example from empiricism—namely, Grounded Theory—and I will eventually contrast its strategies with methods chosen from phenomenology and hermeneutics. But before describing the methods, I shall first give a brief description of the founding philosophies.

## Empiricism, Pragmatism, Symbolic Interactionism, and Constructivism

It seems as though several varieties of empiricism have been cited as the basis for grounded theory. Originally, Glaser and Strauss (1967), without acknowledging any particular philosophy, developed grounded theory on the basis of a standard empirical approach, but in fact what they initially developed was a mixture of Columbia University's positivism (Glaser) and the University of Chicago's pragmatism and symbolic interactionist perspective (Strauss). Later, Charmaz (2000) and Corbin (Corbin & Strauss, 2008) added postmodernist interpretations to the grounded theory approach. But all these different labels refer to varieties of empiricism.

As stated above, empiricism is the oldest philosophy and has served as a basis for science in the West. In modern times, its origins go back to the beginnings of the seventeenth century with the work of Bacon (1561–1626) and Hobbes (1588–1679), and it has morphed into many versions throughout its long history. The key proposition of empiricism is that all knowledge has to be rooted in experience, with special emphasis on sensory modalities. While the precise meaning of experience may be hard to articulate, it implies the notion that whatever is given to it has to be in some sense palpable.

Empiricism is often characterized negatively, in terms of what it denies. It is against forms of a priori truths, against the idea of innate knowledge, against all forms of idealism, and it acknowledges that facts can always be other than the way they were initially ascertained to be. Consequently, subsequent verification, especially by others, is important for establishing solid knowledge, and knowledge claimed by a single individual is deemed to be tentative. Empiricists prefer to reason by induction rather than deduction. Although the latter is not necessarily excluded, empiricists try to come up with general truths based upon individual facts, or else to develop theories based upon a limited number of facts.

The ability to predict future events accurately on the basis of specific hypotheses or general theories is an important criterion for establishing the validity of knowledge. In the course of its history, a form known as logical empiricism developed whereby the reasoning provided by logic and mathematics, two eidetic sciences, were applied to empirical discoveries to help counteract the radical contingency of facts. More specific features of traditional empiricism will be discussed in conjunction with the method that is based upon it.

## Pragmatism

After the appearance of their first publication, Glaser and Strauss became aware of differences in how each of them understood the practice of grounded theory and the philosophy behind it. Glaser (1978; 1992) stayed with a basic empirical approach. However, Strauss, after joining up with Corbin (Corbin & Strauss, 2008), explicitly acknowledged that in working with Corbin his approach could be called pragmatic. The philosophy of pragmatism began with Peirce (1986) and James (1907) and was extended by Mead (Reck, 1964) and Dewey (1973).

Peirce (1986, p. 266) initiated the movement with the famous sentences that expressed the main idea of pragmatism: "Consider what effects, which might conceivably have practical bearings, we conceive the object of our perception to have. Then, our conception of these effects is the whole of our conception of the object." That pragmatism includes empirical criteria is clear from Peirce's (1986, p. 265) statement regarding clarity of thought: "Thus, we come down to what is tangible and practical, as the root of every real distinction of thought, no matter how subtle it may be; and thus there is no distinction of meaning so fine as to consist in anything but a possible difference of practice." Practices are far more palpable than intellectual distinctions.

James followed Peirce's lead. He acknowledged that his sense of pragmatism was based upon Peirce's and agreed with Peirce's idea of clarity of thought when he (James, 1907, pp. 46–47) wrote: "To attain perfect clearness in our thoughts of an object, then, we need only consider what conceivable effects of a practical kind the object may involve—what sensations we are to expect from it, and what reactions we must prepare. Our conception of these effects, whether immediate or remote, is then for us the whole of our conception of the object, so far as that conception has positive significance at all."

Thus, for both Peirce and James, the clarity of a conscious process is based upon all of the implications that can be enumerated, whether imagined or perceived. Buchler (1940, p. xi) has said of Peirce that his type of pragmatism differs "from nineteenth-century positivism, primarily in that it introduces the concept of meaning into empiricist methodology. It is the first deliberate *theory* of meaning in modern times, and it offers a *logical* technique for the clarification of ideas" (italics in original). Peirce maintained that since thought is cognitive, it has to be symbolic in character.

G. H. Mead was another significant contributor to pragmatic philosophy. Miller (1973) reports that Mead moved away from calling his philosophy "functionalism" because he wanted to emphasize that his philosophy was based upon a behavioristic theory. Miller (p. xxix) explains: "This he did for the reason that the earlier functional psychology did not emphasize sufficiently either the *social* character of *behavior* or the behavioral character of mind and reflective thinking" (italics in original). Miller also explains that Mead was not a behaviorist like Watson or Skinner because he did not reduce mind to observable behavior but insisted on explaining mental phenomena in terms of overt behavior. Miller (p. 69) summarized Mead's position when he said, "Extreme behaviorists are correct in denying the existence of consciousness and mind as spiritual stuff, but they are wrong in denying its existence altogether, or in believing that it cannot be explained in relation to observable behavior." In all these views, there is no basic departure from an empirical type of thinking.

The remaining key developer of pragmatism was John Dewey. The innovations he brought to pragmatism were creative but wholly in line with empiricism. Dewey's (1973) view was that "Pragmatism, thus, presents itself as an extension of historical empiricism, but with this fundamental difference, that it does not insist upon antecedent phenomena but upon consequent phenomena; not upon the precedents but upon the possibilities of action" (p. 50). It is known that empiricism emphasizes the study of experience, and in the beginning the exact focus of pragmatism was unclear, so Dewey set out to help clarify matters. Dewey (1998a) wrote:

> The criticisms made upon that vital but still unformed movement variously termed radical empiricism, pragmatism, humanism, functionalism, according to as one or another aspect of it is uppermost, have left me with a conviction that the *fundamental* difference is not so much in matters overtly discussed as in a presupposition that remains tacit: a presupposition as to what experience is and means.... Immediate empiricism postulates that things—anything, everything, in the ordinary or non-technical use of the term "thing"—are what they are experienced as. Hence, if one wishes to describe anything truly, his task is to tell what it is experienced as being. (p. 115)

Being a creative thinker, Dewey wanted to emphasize his own meaning of experience. He felt that traditional empiricism referred too much to past events and antecedents. Dewey (1998b, p. 48) wrote, "...but experience in its vital form is experimental, an effort to change the given; it is characterized by projection, by reaching forward into the unknown; connexion with a future is its salient trait." Thus, Dewey radically extended the understanding of experience, but insofar as he emphasized it he was in the camp of empirical philosophy.

## Symbolic Interactionism

Symbolic Interactionism is also within the purview of empirical philosophy. However, symbolic interactionism is not so much a philosophy as a theoretical scientific perspective designed to guide empirical research with social phenomena. Herbert Blumer (1969) is the person who articulated the position most systematically and has stated that he relies chiefly on the thought of Mead, whom we saw above was an acknowledged empiricist. Blumer (1969, p. 2) articulates three premises as the basis for symbolic interactionism: (1) "... human beings act toward things on the basis of the meanings that the things have for them," (2) "... the meaning of such things....arises out of the social interaction that one has with one's fellows," and (3) "...these meanings are handled in, and modified through, an interpretive process used by the person in dealing with the things he encounters." However, these premises are meant to be entirely empirical in character as Blumer (1969) went on to say:

> The principles that comprise the methodology of an empirical science have to cover the act of scientific inquiry, not in some detached logical form of its own, but in the form that such scientific inquiry must take in grappling with a given kind of empirical world....Every part of the act of scientific inquiry— and hence the full act itself—is subject to the test of the empirical world and has to be validated through such a test. (p. 17)

Most explicitly, Blumer (1969) wrote, "My concern is limited to that form of social theory which stands or presumes to stand as a part of empirical science" (p. 140). While Blumer's methodological perspective is much more liberal than that of empirical positivists, he is still nevertheless guided by empirical principles.

## Constructivism

Constructivism is also not so much a philosophy as a theoretical perspective encouraging a certain orientation toward data. Charmaz (2000, p. 510) first articulated this postmodernist interpretation of grounded theory procedures in print when she stated that "Constructivism assumes the relativism of multiple social realities, recognizes the mutual creation of knowledge by the viewer and the viewed, and aims toward interpretive understanding of subjects' meanings." Her views also influenced the perspective of Corbin (Corbin & Straus, 2008), who admitted that:

> There is no doubt that I, Corbin, have been influenced to some degree by the writings of contemporary feminists, constructionists, and postmodernists. I especially admire the works of both Clarke (2005) and Charmaz (2006) and how they have applied postmodernist and postcontructivist paradigms to *grounded theory* methodology, thus taking up the challenge of Denzin (1994, p. 512) to move interpretive *methods* more deeply into the regions of postmodern sensibility. (p. 9)

Thus, the recent modifications to grounded theory procedural strategies pull them even further away from the original strategies as understood by Glaser (1992), whom Charmaz (2000, p. 510) views as a basic positivist. Despite the looser strategies advocated by Charmaz and Corbin, the approach is still basically empirical. Charmaz (2000, p. 509) writes that "Essentially, grounded theory methods consist of systematic inductive guidelines for collecting and analyzing data to build middle range theoretical frameworks that explain the collected data" and that "Constructivist grounded theory celebrates firsthand knowledge of empirical worlds..." (Charmaz, 2000, p. 510). It should also be noted that the very idea of construction has been part of empirical approaches for a long time (Blumer, 1969), but it is the postmodern interpretation of what it means that is novel.

## Grounded Theory

One of the earliest qualitative methods developed in recent times is grounded theory as initially developed by Glaser and Strauss (1967). As previously noted, developments have taken place since its initial exposition. While it began in sociology, the use of its procedures has extended to other disciplines as well since it was designed to be a generic method (Glaser, 1978, p. 164). Grounded theory, as its name implies, has as its task the generation of theory on the basis of data rather than on the exclusive basis of speculative thinking. It emphasizes qualitative discriminations, although quantitative analyses are not ruled out. The basic process is to use comparative analysis, which should lead to theoretical sampling. Comparative analysis is a process whereby the reading of the data suggests categories or hypotheses that begin to form a theory concerning the data being analyzed. It is a tentative process in which the emerging categories (self-standing concepts) and properties (conceptual aspects of categories) are tested against the ongoing reading of the data.

Our interest here is to show how the steps are everywhere guided by the criteria of empirical philosophy. I will first list the practical steps that the grounded theorist undertakes and then elaborate on the empirical criteria or values being followed. Because each author presents them slightly differently and in elaborate ways, I will give a generic list of the procedures as provided by Charmaz (2014), who provides us with a very succinct description of them. According to Charmaz (2014, pp. 7–8) the basic steps of grounded theory procedures are:

1. Simultaneous involvement in data collection and analysis
2. Constructing analytic codes and categories from data, not from preconceived logically deduced hypotheses
3. Using the constant comparative method, which involves making comparisons during each stage of the analysis
4. Advancing theory development during each step of data collection and analysis
5. Memo-writing to elaborate categories, specify their properties, define relationships between categories, and identify gaps
6. Sampling aimed at theory construction, not for population representativeness
7. Conducting the literature review *after* developing an independent analysis (italics in original)

**Empirical Criteria Guiding the Procedures of Grounded Theory**
Grounded theory's first methodical steps are: 1) simultaneous involvement in data collection and analysis, and, 2) constructing analytic codes and categories from data. These first two steps cannot be easily separated, so they will be considered together. Data, of course, is collected, usually in the form of description of experiences, and the

researcher begins to analyze the data before it is determined that enough data has been collected. The type of additional data to be obtained depends on the theory that is forming. The chief outcome of this early phase of analysis is the establishment of strict data-dependent codes and categories. All articulated concepts and properties must have a basis in the data.

With these steps, the researcher begins by reading descriptive data provided by others and starts making tentative comparisons and distinctions that she finds in the data from a psychological perspective, possibly even generating her first theoretical hypotheses. Empirically, the ability to make distinctions and comparisons is acknowledged; because they can be repeated and are to some extent justified, although precisely how such distinctions and comparisons are made is not addressed. It is taken for granted. Glaser and Strauss (1967) admit that a key element in the process of developing theory is achieving insights. But the insights have to come from a professional, disciplinary perspective. Glaser & Strauss write, "This book is intended to underscore the basic sociological activity that *only* sociologists can do; generating sociological theory…. Only sociologists are trained to want it, to look for it, and to generate it" (pp. 6–7). Of course, trained psychologists would adopt the psychological perspective.

Glaser (1978) emphasizes that the theory developed from the data has to be an emerging theory, and he recommends certain procedures to foster theoretical sensitivity. Glaser first suggests that one analyze "with as few predetermined ideas as possible—especially logically deducted, a prior (sic) hypotheses" (p. 3). He also suggests that the researcher be steeped in the literature to gain familiarity with the variables and ideas that belong to a given substantive area. Furthermore, Glaser states that the emergent theory must have fit, relevance, be modifiable, and work. All of these criteria are correlated with theoretical sensitivity. That is, the theoretically sensitive researcher will be better able to make such judgments. While examples are given, precisely what processes one must go through to achieve the desired results are not offered. This is probably because empiricism hesitates to enter into the conscious processes involved in such activities.

The initial relationships suggested by the data and perceived by the researcher are called hypotheses—in part because the analytic process is not completed and therefore the developing theory could change and also because the discriminations are so far, usually, the result of a solitary analyzer. Empiricism considers any judgment based upon a single observer to be tentative. This may help explain why the outcome of the research process is a theory. In other words, the user of this method does not describe findings, or even underlying structures of the experiences studied, but rather comes up with theories that can possibly explain what took place. In general, the strength of empiricism is in establishing facts. However, there is not much significance attached to the establishment of a single fact. Rather, it is the relationship among several facts that is important, and this relationship begins hypothetically or as a theory. Consequently, in grounded theory insights replace facts, and the relationships among insights is the beginning of theorizing. Grounded theorists believe that establishing insights close to the data is superior to speculative thinking when it comes to developing theories, but they do not articulate how the insights are derived from the facts upon which they are based.

Glaser (2003) strongly advocates conceptualization as opposed to description, an additional advantage being that "conceptualizations producing conceptual hypotheses save the research from the worrisome accuracy problem" (p. 85). It is asserted that the conceptualization is based on the data, but then it is not clear why the conceptualizations remain hypothetical. If the conceptual expression is hypothetical, how is speculation removed? In other words, more work seems to be necessary to distinguish conceptualization, which Glaser claims to be doing, from speculation, which he eschews. In any case, conceptualization is directly related to the hypothetical-deductive method advocated by empiricism. With this procedure, one first hypothesizes an explanation about an event and then gathers data to see if the hypothesis is confirmed. (With grounded theory an immediate verification of the hypothesis or theory is not sought.) The integration of a series of hypotheses becomes a theory. The theory then guides further data collection to see how well the theory stands up or to determine in what ways it must be modified to be faithful to the increasing amount of data.

To take an example, Glaser and Strauss (1967) describe how they came up with the category of "social loss" in their work with dying patients. They write:

> For example, the category of "social loss" of dying patients emerged quickly from comparison of nurses' responses to the potential deaths of their patients. Each relevant response involved the nurse's appraisal of the degree of loss that her patient would be to his family, his occupation, or society: "He

was so young." "He was to be a doctor." "She had a full life" or "What will the children and her husband do without her?" (pp. 105–106)

The above enumerated expressions became the basis for the sociological category of "social loss." How or why the sociologists came up with that particular category is not addressed. It's true that a critic can review the data and the outcome and determine whether or not it is plausible. But the critic's process is wholly independent of that of the original researcher. On one hand, different researchers using different processes and arriving at the same result is good. On the other hand, no one is enlightened concerning the processes whereby a good result is achieved. Ultimately, the grounded theorist can assert that his insight is hypothetical, part of a theory, and thus susceptible to further verification or modification.

It is important to notice a difference that empirical qualitative analyses introduce. In the initial empirical psychological studies (not including introspective studies), a measured physical fact was usually correlated with the experience of a participant. Thus, a light flickering at the rate of 70 cycles per second is experienced as fused by a participant. In such a case, a strictly measured physical event is correlated with an experience. If the stimuli were not strictly measured, then the conditions were strictly controlled (e.g., mazes) or materials were strictly measured (nonsense syllables had specific association values).

However, with grounded theory analyses, rather open-ended linguistic expressions depicting some everyday meaning are correlated with disciplinary theoretical insights expressing a different, but presumably allied, meaning. The scientific effort here involves the transformation of one kind of meaning for another. Specifically, particular meanings from one perspective (everyday life) are transformed into a more general meaning in another perspective (disciplinary perspective). The logic of this process is rarely spoken to.

The fact that one begins to analyze data soon after it is obtained, or before all of it is obtained, is not really a problem in terms of scientific methodology. What matters is the accuracy with which the analysis is done.

In addition to steps one and two—simultaneous involvement in data collection and analysis, and construction of analytic codes and categories from data—grounded theory's remaining methodical steps are: 3) using the constant comparative method, which involves making comparisons during each stage of the analysis; 4) advancing theory development during each step of data collection and analysis; 5) memo-writing to elaborate categories, specify their properties, define relationships between categories, and identify gaps; and 6) sampling aimed at theory construction.

Since the remaining steps are not necessarily sequential but activities that can be done alternatively, we can also treat them together. In a certain sense, discrete steps are assigned to different tasks in what would otherwise be a seamless activity. Ultimately, all these procedures participate in the development of theory. The use of the constant comparative method begins with the coding of each incident in the data, and initially at least many coding categories are encouraged. Coding means that one uses a shorthand term to designate what the incident is about, which is not a simple association but should be the result of discriminatory and analytic processes. The code begins to intimate what the theory will become.

The rule that guides the constant comparative method, according to Glaser and Strauss (1967), is: "*while coding an incident for a category, compare it with the previous incidents in the same and different groups coded in the same category*" (p. 106; italics in original). As the coding and comparisons continue, one begins to integrate categories and properties and thus discovers that the process of theory generation has already begun. It is at this point that it may prove useful to do some memo writing so that the developing theory can become more explicit. The memo then becomes the written record of the analysis (Corbin & Strauss, 2008). During the course of the memo writing, the researcher may experience the need for theoretical sampling in order to gain some deeper understanding about the emerging theory. According to Corbin and Strauss (2008), theoretical sampling is "Data gathering based on evolving concepts. The idea is to look for situations that would bring out the varying properties and dimensions of a concept" (p. 117).

As one looks at the conscious processes that take place within these steps, there is a certain constancy: In the face of the data the researcher is confronting, she must make discriminatory judgments and articulate them. Whether coding, comparing, creating categories or properties, initially articulating a theory, or writing a memo, the researcher must come up with linguistic expressions that depict the empirical data in a disciplinary, theoretically sensitive way. Since the codes, the categories, the properties and the theories are all generated (developed, constructed) by the researcher, to what extent can one say that the results are empirical? Yes, the researcher confronts some empirical data, but the data are originally expressed in everyday or non-disciplinary terms and during the analysis the everyday terms take on a psychological (disciplinary) meaning. What is the relationship between the everyday terms and the psychological (disciplinary) expression that is ultimately used? In what sense is the disciplinary expression an empirical one?

With this method one begins by reflecting on the obtained data and forms concepts and properties on the basis of a disciplined, theoretically sensitive perspective. Consequently, a certain transformation of the original data takes place as well as data reduction with the use of coding. Empirical data usually expressed in the non-disciplinary language of everyday life are expressed in terms loaded with psychological (disciplinary) meanings; phrases and expressions that are sentence length or longer are reduced because of coding to a single word or short phrases also conveying psychological (disciplinary) meaning. The processes employed to accomplish these goals are not addressed, but the results are available so that a critical other can potentially evaluate the outcomes. The activities correlated with the remaining steps of the method—advancing theory development, memo writing, and theoretical sampling—are also primarily researcher generated even if originally data dependent. It also should be noted that the descriptions are typically obtained without any independent check on the situations being described, so that they are usually trusted as obtained.

Although this procedure has a long tradition in social science research and is an acceptable practice, it introduces a possible source of vulnerability. It seems that only Glaser (2003) exempts himself from this vulnerability by saying that grounded theory emphasizes conceptualization and not description. Conceptualization abstracts from time, place, and persons in a way that description does not. Moreover, the results of the process are "emergent conceptual categories and their properties integrated into hypotheses" (Glaser, 2003, p. 51) that eventually become theories. As theories, they are held to be tentative until proven.

Thus, an empirically based qualitative method as exemplified by grounded theory basically seeks the lived meanings expressed by individuals living in various contexts in everyday life in order to provide a theoretical, disciplinary understanding of the same event. In order to build a theory, the researcher must transform the detected everyday meanings into disciplinary meanings. The raw data is clearly empirical, but the insights based upon the empirical data are as much determined by the disciplinary stance as by the empirical data. This can be problematic for not yet well-established disciplines like psychology because one could interpret the everyday empirical meanings psychoanalytically, behaviorally, or cognitively and still be justified as a psychological interpreter. Thus, grounded theory is more empirically based than purely empirical but, as practiced, it is nevertheless a legitimate scientific perspective.

## Hermeneutics: Context and Philosophy

Hermeneutics did not begin as a philosophy but it evolved into one. It began as a set of rules and procedures for interpreting biblical passages and evolved into a theory concerning methodical procedures for investigating human science phenomena and, beyond that, into a philosophy articulating how to comprehend the phenomenon of "understanding" as such (Palmer, 1969). It was Schleiermacher who made the first synthesis of different interpretive procedures that were applied to different texts (Ricoeur, 1981), and Dilthey (1977) who articulated a methodical procedure for research in the human sciences. These procedures were further enhanced by Betti (1955), Hirsch (1967), Ricoeur (1981) and Taylor (1985). Finally, it was Heidegger (1962) and Gadamer (1975) who established hermeneutics as a philosophical procedure for comprehending the mode of being of "understanding."

Unlike in empirical philosophy, where different names were given to varied procedures and presuppositions, the name hermeneutics is given to different modes and levels of interpretive analysis—even to a blurring of the distinction between philosophy and the social sciences (Rabinow & Sullivan, 1987). This condition leads to a diversity of methodical procedures used by social scientists to which the term "hermeneutic method" is applied. Consequently, the selection of a procedure that might be common to psychological researchers is a difficult task, and I'm not at all sure that such a commonality exists. I have chosen the book by Packer and Addison (1989) as the basic text to speak about the application of hermeneutics to psychology because it claims to contain many examples of interpretive research in the realm of psychology.

All hermeneutic researchers believe that human phenomena have to be interpreted in order to be understood. One implication of this stance is that the best knowledge to be had is a plausible understanding of a phenomenon rather than a definitive, objective understanding that leaves no room for alternatives, such as knowledge that can be obtained in the sciences of nature. What has to be interpreted is a text or a text-analogue. Such texts or text-analogues are produced by human subjects, who bring a complex perspective to the text or analogue, introducing the problem of context and frequently expressing the texts in language that brings in the problem of polysemy (Ricoeur, 1981a). Polysemy refers to the many meanings words can have outside of the context. The presence of context introduces many problems: the question of the author's intent, the audience to whom the author is speaking, how well the author expressed his intent and so on. Consequently, unlike natural phenomena that are ruled by causes and effects independent of humans, determinations influenced by subjectivity prevail everywhere with human phenomena. For these thinkers there is no alternative but to interpret.

One reason the universality of interpretation is posited is that all hermeneutic researchers agree that one must conduct research from within the hermeneutic circle. When one uses the hermeneutic circle, the assumption is that there is no independent starting point for research with human phenomena. The goal in such research is to understand lived experiences through the expressed meanings contained in those experiences. As Palmer (1969) puts it, "The whole receives its definition from the parts, and reciprocatedly, the parts can only be understood in reference to the whole" (p. 118). Palmer goes on to state, following Dilthey, that "...meaning is what understanding grasps in the essential reciprocal interaction of the whole and its parts" (p. 118). This idea is analogically applied to life experiences and directly to texts. While hermeneutic reasoning has a circular quality, it is always claimed that that the logic is appropriate and does not constitute a vicious circle. The ultimate consequence is that the theory of scientific research with human phenomena is radically different from the theory governing the material phenomena of nature (Gadamer, 1987).

## Hermeneutic Method

As indicated above, a hermeneutic method has been practiced since at least the eighteenth century. It is an intrinsically qualitative method that seeks the meaning of texts or text-analogues that are in some way initially obscure or ambiguous. There appears to be great variability in how it is practiced, but the essential elements seem to be (1) that the researcher comes up with the best interpreted meaning of the text (or text-analogue), the implication being that the result is not without other possible understandings, although the positing of a truth claim is not ruled out (Packer & Addison, 1989a, pp. 278–279), and (2) that the analysis requires the use of the hermeneutic circle with its fore-structures of understanding. At least, these are the steps that can be gleamed from the expositions by Packer and Addison (1989b, pp. 13–38; 1989a, pp. 278–292). Addison and Packer both provided examples of hermeneutic psychological research using the above two enumerated steps. Addison (1989, p. 39) described the steps he went through to complete his interpretive research as those in which he was sensitive to "the relationship between immersion, understanding, and interpretation, the fore-structure of interpretation, the background context, and how interpretive accounts can open up possibilities." Packer (1989) used the analysis of videotapes as his data base for studying moral conflicts. Packer also basically immersed himself in the data, emphasized the role of the fore-structure of interpretation and the use of the hermeneutic circle, and deliberated over the place in the data to enter the circle properly. In addition, he emphasized that the desirable outcome of the study would be to change the reality of what was studied for the better and not simply to report the findings.[1]

Strangely, only one other article in Packer and Addison's (1989) book was explicitly hermeneutic in the sense that the two criteria posited above were explicitly used. This was the article by Brown, Tappan, Gilligan, Miller, and Argyris (1989).[2] Their study is complex in the sense that they wanted to understand two moral voices: that of justice and that of care. In developing their hermeneutic method, the authors state that they were guided by the work of Mishler, Dilthey and Ricoeur. They explicitly adopted the hermeneutic circle as part of their method and were concerned that their interpretations were valid. Brown et al. used an open-ended clinical interview to collect their data, and a series of questions was provided to help the interviewer focus on specific issues. They then developed a Reading Guide that helped them track the voice of the person as well as the two moral voices of justice and care. Finally, they read the texts multiple times because "Each reading serves to identify a different aspect of the narrative deemed relevant in locating self and ascertaining moral voice" (1989, p. 148). The first reading of the narrative was simply to establish the story, and the subsequent three readings were to interpret the self, the care voice and the justice voice. Brown and colleagues also attempted to establish the reliability and validity of their results according to hermeneutic theory but not according to standard psychometric practices.

In his analysis, Packer (Packer & Addison, 1989, p. 96) claims to be guided by Heidegger's ontological method, even though he applied Heideggerian insights at the ontical level. Packer does not detail just how he transformed Heidegger's ontological analyses into an ontical analysis or method, but simply articulates the ideas that he used and how he applied them. It appears that Packer used the hermeneutic method as basically formulated by Dilthey but selectively used Heideggerian ontological terms to elaborate his findings.

However, it is important not to confuse ontical and ontological levels because at the ontological level the application of hermeneutics was not about method. Gadamer (1975) has written:

> I did not intend to produce an art or technique of understanding, in the manner of the earlier hermeneutics. I did not wish to elaborate a system of rules to describe, let alone direct, the methodical procedures of the human sciences. Nor was it my aim to investigate the theoretical foundation of work in these fields in order to put my findings to practical ends. (p. xvi)

Gadamer (1987, p. 130) attributes the same concern to Heidegger, saying,

> Under these circumstances we will understand why the task of hermeneutics as described by Heidegger is not a simple matter of recommending a method. Quite the contrary, he demands nothing less than a radical account of actual understanding as everyone who understands has always accomplished it. (p. 130)

Ricoeur (1981a) makes the same argument. Commenting on Heidegger, he writes:

> Consequently, to display the constitution of Dasein is not at all "to ground by derivation", as in the methodology of the human sciences, but "to unfold the foundation by clarification" (see SZ para. 3). An opposition is thus established between ontological foundation, in the sense just described, and epistemological grounding.... What is at stake in philosophical hermeneutics will thus be "the explication of those beings with regard to their basic state of being" (SZ 10; BT 30). This explication will add nothing to the methodology of the human sciences; rather it will

dig beneath this methodology in order to lay bare its foundations. (pp. 54–55)

The transformation of hermeneutics from epistemology to ontology surely has implications for epistemology, but it is something that needs to be worked out thoroughly rather than merely assumed or applied in an ad hoc manner.

## Criteria to Which Hermeneutic Methods Must Adhere

While there are many variations and amendations in the practice of the hermeneutic method, it is absolutely critical that two features be maintained: (1) explicit use of the hermeneutic circle with its attendant practices, and (2) the best possible interpretation, which usually is sought with the help of auxiliary procedures. By attendant practices in the first step, I mean things like determining the proper place to enter the circle, establishing an authentic way of entering the circle, and considering the role of the fore-structure of thought (Packer, 1989). Auxiliary procedures allied with the second step include the evaluative approaches detailed by Packer and Addison (1989) that help secure an interpretation, even though they do not provide a final proof. Implicit in the expression "best possible outcome" is the idea that not all alternative interpretations are eliminated. They are simply deemed not to be as good as the best possible interpretation. Although not explicitly stated by Packer and Addison (1989a; 1989b), their expositions lead to the conclusion that the above two criteria are necessary for methodical interpretive practices.

If we use the above two criteria, it is clear that not all of the articles assembled by Packer and Addison (1989) in their collection can be called genuine examples of methodical interpretive research. This does not mean that the articles are not good. Indeed, some are excellent. I simply mean that they do not explicitly follow the criteria mentioned above. Consequently, of the eleven articles in the collection, only three are true examples of methodical interpretive analyses: the expositions of hermeneutics written by the two editors, Addison (1989) and Packer (1989), where the criteria I posited are mentioned and discussed, and the article written by Brown, Tappan, Gilligan, Miller and Argyris (1989). What is common to these three articles, which actually applied methodical interpretive procedures, is that original data was collected and systematically analyzed in each of them.[3] Consequently, the opportunity to implement the hermeneutic method fully was present.

The authors of the book's remaining eight articles either had already collected data or employed purposes that did not require new data.

I want to make clear that I do not think that every published article has to follow the procedures demanded of articles that produce original research. There are many types of articles: Some are theoretical, some are analyses of practices, some provide summaries of ongoing research, some are critical of prevailing attitudes, and so forth. These different types of articles have different standards of rigor and should not be judged by the single standard of articles publishing original research. However, the collection assembled by Packer and Addison (1989) is meant to be an exemplar of how interpretive research should be conducted, so one would expect most of the articles to meet the minimal criteria.

A problem with the articles that do not collect original data is that they are hard to differentiate from scientific articles in general. It has to be acknowledged that any scientific evaluation of ordinary phenomena that take place in everyday life results in an interpretation of the Lifeworld event. So, a psychological evaluation of criminal behavior, the diagnosis of abnormal behavior, the pedagogical analysis of teacher performance, a grammatical analysis of public speaking, etc., all result in interpretations of Lifeworld events. In such cases, a specialized, disciplinary perspective that has some degree of arbitrariness to it with respect to the chosen event is applied to an everyday event, and a new account of the event based on the disciplinary perspective is produced. That is, the event chosen usually does not have to be the event for examining the chosen phenomenon, but certain contingent factors also enter in to make that particular event a convenient one to be analyzed. Thus, the disciplinary analysis and account become an interpretation of the Lifeworld event, providing a specialized and limited understanding of a richer, more complex lived event. The event has then been interpreted. In this sense, even quantitative studies become interpretations.

I bring up the above sense of interpretation because the articles in Packer and Addison's (1989) collection that I did not mention are interpretive only in that sense. That is, the articles that I did not designate as interpretive are not methodically interpretive in the sense of explicitly using the hermeneutic circle and/or procedures to test the strength of the best interpretation. They are interpretive only in the sense that all scientific studies are interpretive and not in the special sense that hermeneutic studies employ an explicitly well-defined interpretive method. In fact, a strong case can be made that the article by Spence (1989) is an example of a descriptive method rather than an interpretive one. Spence described the criteria for identifying a study as being scientific and then carefully described the steps followed by a psychoanalytic researcher who used a case study method, vividly demonstrating that the case study researcher did not follow the explicitly described scientific criteria. Of course, the result was not a genuinely scientific reinterpretation of the case study but used a method of analysis that was descriptive and not interpretive.

Finally, it is rather clear that part of the background understanding that Packer and Addison bring to their studies is the idea of hermeneutic universalism, although it is not made explicit. Hermeneutic universalism assumes that all expressions have to be interpreted. This means that a distinction between interpretation and description is not upheld, even though some form of the word "description" is used by each editor. However, key hermeneutic philosophers admit that there are conditions for the use of interpretation. For example, both Gadamer (1975, p. 90) and Taylor (1985, p. 150) have stated that in order for an interpretation to be undertaken the initial situation has to be in some sense obscure, ambiguous, or unclear. If obscurity is lacking, the demand to interpret is not present. Consequently, not every encounter with a text or text-analogue calls for an interpretation, and where interpretations are not called for, descriptions are performed. This is a critical distinction that the editors have overlooked.

Overall then, hermeneutics has always been interested in the clarification of expressed meanings. As a method geared toward psychological research, it is interested in clarifying psychological meanings. Just how psychological meanings are discriminated from general meanings has not yet been fully clarified. While it has taken a different route, the hermeneutic methodical project is the same as that of empiricism: to detect and clarify everyday lived meanings as expressed by human persons and to transform them into more precise disciplinary meanings. Because of the assumptions underlying their procedures, hermeneutic results are interpretations, which also implies that they are not definitive. In that sense, they could also be understood as theories because of their tentativeness.

## Phenomenology

The remaining philosophy and method to be considered is Husserlian phenomenology, which employs a descriptive approach. This perspective is based on the philosophy of Edmund Husserl, the founder of phenomenology. Phenomenological philosophy was initiated in 1900 with the publication of *Logical Investigations* by Husserl (1970a), who then radically transformed his approach with the publication of *Ideas I* (Husserl, 1983) in 1913 and again with the publication of *The Crisis of European Sciences and Transcendental Phenomenology* (Husserl, 1970b).

Husserlian phenomenology's approach to consciousness is philosophical and epistemological. Because Husserl assumes a transcendental attitude toward consciousness, Husserlian results refer to consciousness as such, and not to any specific form of consciousness. An additional value of his transcendental approach is that he was able to provide a philosophical articulation of consciousness and subjectivity (Husserl, 1978). Up until his writings, the approach to consciousness and subjectivity in philosophy had been empirical. Even though empiricism is a philosophy, it was one in which the appeal to consciousness and subjectivity remained psychological because the reference was always to the functioning of a human or animal consciousness. All of Husserl's analyses performed at the transcendental level are strictly philosophical because they deal with consciousness per se and not with human levels or modes of consciousness and subjectivity.

Only when one uses the phenomenological psychological reduction (Husserl, 1977) as opposed to the transcendental, does one refer to human consciousness and subjectivity and thus to psychological reality. Husserl always remained descriptive in his approach whenever it was possible to do so. Interpretation was for him a default position. The main reason is that for Husserl intuition, i.e., how phenomena present themselves to acts of consciousness, is the basis for knowledge acquisition. The modes of appearance of all objects were meant to be described, and with the help of free imaginative variation their essences were meant to be discovered and communicated also through careful description. This position is not reducible to metaphysics of presence because included among the givens are absences, indeterminancies, and horizons whose farthest edges are obscure. Only in the absence of givens, or with the presence of obscure givens, would interpretation be called for.

Husserl frequently employed the philosophical phenomenological method he developed. It consists of three basic steps: first, experience or imagine a concrete phenomenon and carefully describe it; second, systematically but freely vary dimensions of the phenomenon in order to ascertain its essential features; and, third, describe the essence that has been discovered once the method of free imaginative variation has been completed. This is also known as the eidetic reduction of the concrete phenomenon that was initially experienced. Since Husserl's method is philosophical, any strict application of this method will produce philosophical results. As psychologists, we desire results that are psychological and scientific, not philosophical; consequently, some modifications were made to Husserl's method in order to produce results that are scientific and psychological.

The justification for these modifications has been published elsewhere (see Giorgi, 2009), so we will only list the modified steps here. The scientific phenomenological method encompasses the following steps: (1) One obtains a description of a concrete experience from participants; (2) One then assumes the attitude of the phenomenological psychological reduction as well as an attitude that is sensitive to the phenomenon being researched; (3) One reads the description provided by the participant in order to get a sense of the whole; (4) The researcher then rereads the description and establishes meaning units—i.e., parts of the description that have a relatively coherent sense; (5) One then transforms the meaning units into phenomenological and psychologically sensitive expressions; (6) Finally, the researcher integrates the data and uses free imaginative variation to help determine the psychological essence of the experience. This essence is eidetic, but it is not universal. It is only general because psychological experiences tend to group according to typologies and thus do not comprehend the whole field of experience of the specific phenomenon being investigated.

## Phenomenological Philosophical Criteria Guiding Phenomenological Analyses

The ultimate outcome of phenomenological analyses are eidetic expressions concerning the meaning of experiential events. What phenomenology adds to normal scientific analyses are the probings into subjective acts that are the correlates of worldly presentations. Husserl admits that the acts correlated with objective presentations are usually performed unconsciously and thus require careful reflective practices to bring them to light, where possible, and to describe them. While philosophical results are usually expressed in universal terms, scientific eidetic findings remain general because they usually result in typological categories that fall short of universality. But findings that are essentially typical are proper scientific results.

The results of the application of the scientific phenomenological method are eidetic descriptions that are general and based upon intuitions that are clarified with the help of the procedure of imaginative variation. It is understood that the eidetic structures that are produced comprehend multiple empirical variations. They express the unified understanding that makes possible the clustering of all the empirical instances of a certain type.

In general, phenomenological philosophy is identified by five characteristics: apriority, eideticism, intuition, intentionality, and transcendentality. Phenomenological psychology accepts all these features but modifies some in order to meet scientific rather than philosophical criteria. It accepts intuition and intentionality the same way as phenomenological philosophy does. It is not transcendental because it chooses to understand either actual human or animal consciousness rather than a transcendentally purified consciousness, but such modes of consciousness are still to be studied within a type of phenomenological reduction. It is eidetic, but its findings are general rather than universal because they express typicalities. Finally, it is often quasi a priori because the attainment of empirical data often limits the extension of the a priori involvement. In other words, the a priori feature is still there, but its extension is sometimes limited by the empirical typology of the data.

## Comparison of Philosophies

Since each method basically follows the dictates of the philosophy it adopts, it makes more sense to compare the philosophies rather than the methods themselves in order to see the relative strengths of each approach. The following analyses present the primary values of each philosophy according to its own criteria. Later, an evaluative analysis of the philosophies will be undertaken.

**Empiricism.** As we saw, empiricism comes in many forms. In its most fundamental form, empiricism states that all knowledge is based upon, or derived from, experience. Issues arise when one tries to clarify the nature of experience itself, as well as the types of objects that can be given to it, in part because the ontological status of consciousness is dubious in empiricism. One clear acceptable meaning is that experience is the presentation of anything that can be given via the senses. The correlate of this notion is the idea of palpability—i.e., the notion that whatever is given to experience must have some type of sensorial delineation in order to be considered a genuine given. It is hard to find direct confirmation of this idea, but Peirce, cited by Rosensohn (1974) expressed it well when he wrote: "Philosophy ought to imitate the successful sciences so far as to proceed only from *tangible* premises which can be subjected to careful scrutiny..." (p. 29, emphasis added). Historically, this task was easy because empiricism's strength was in determining facts, and except for introspective studies the facts were always external. Empiricism was concerned with how stable the facts were and with detecting how the facts varied with varied conditions.

However, with grounded theory, in all of its empirical forms, a certain shift has taken place whereby objectively measured facts have been replaced by meaningful linguistic expressions as indicators of a subjective attitude. These expressions are mined for their disciplinary significance, and researchers then express their original findings in terms of "categories," "codes," "theoretical concepts," "properties," and so on. These notions become the nuclei around which psychological (or other disciplinary) theories are to be described. Everything now takes place on the level of meaning. The meanings expressed in the original descriptions are transformed into the meaningful categories of the discipline.

The form of empiricism under which Glaser and the early Strauss (before he teamed up with Corbin) worked make this clear. They (Glaser & Strauss, 1967, p. 6) wrote: "Generating a theory from data means that most hypotheses and concepts not only come from the data but are systematically worked out in relation to the data during the course of the research." But Strauss did not mention in his statement that the end result is a transformation of the data. Strauss (1987, p. 11) also stated that grounded theory analyses involve the typical empirical procedures of "induction, deduction, and verification." According to Strauss (1987, p. 6), grounded theory analyses also involved "...grasping the actors' viewpoints for understanding interaction, process, and social change." The attempt to grasp the actor's viewpoint means that the empiricism involved with grounded theory is different from the positivistic empiricism that deals with objective facts because it involves interrogating the meanings expressed by persons in order to ascertain the subjective attitude that produced those meanings. It also entails the task of discriminating among the meanings expressed by human subjects in order to attach a disciplinary meaning to the originally expressed everyday meanings.

Since the conscious processes that the empirical researcher goes through to achieve these goals are never revealed, a critic has only the outcomes of the processes to rely on. Consequently, not only is the project an interpretive one—one understands a rich, complex Lifeworld event in terms of a disciplinary perspective with its own concepts and values—but the method is also interpretive. We know what the participant said and then we see the disciplinary meaning that the researcher assigns to it, but we are not aware of how the assignation was accomplished. When dealing with the descriptions of others, all the forms of empiricism employ an interpretive method except the one employed by Glaser—and possibly early Glaser and Strauss.

That all the other forms of the empirical method employ an interpretive component is not hard to document. Strauss (1987), writing on his own without Glaser, explicitly states *"Analysis* is synonymous with *interpretation* of data" (p. 4). While Peirce, Mead, and Dewey were all more philosophers than scientific practitioners, they nevertheless adopted the experimental method as the ideal for solid knowledge and theorized that neither individual subjectivity nor consciousness, nor any other form of intuitive process, had a vital role in the production of knowledge. They did not deny the existence of those phenomena but wanted to account for knowledge independently of them. As empiricists, these philosophers held social theories of meaning that required interpretations to clarify them. Peirce actually had an interpretant theory of meaning; Mead's philosophy of act is thoroughly social, and the understanding of its meaning implies communicability and interpretation. For Dewey events also acquire meaning through communication, implying interpretation.

The person who applied pragmatic philosophy most consistently in a scientific way was Herbert Blumer, who demonstrated that symbolic interactionism was completely concerned with meanings. The premises of symbolic interactionism are that "human beings act toward things on the basis of the meanings that things have for them...and that the meanings of such things... arise out of social interaction that one has with one's fellows...and these meanings are modified through an interpretive process used by the person in dealing with these encounters" (Blumer, 1969, p. 2). But then the results of the research imply that the researcher needs to interpret his findings because the scientist "has to relate his findings to an outside body of theory or to a set of conceptions that transcend the study he has made" (Blumer, 1969, p. 26). Throughout symbolic interactionist research, no role is given for subjective intuitive processes in the assessment of meanings.

Under the title of constructivism, the grounded theory method, while remaining empirical, gets a bit more varied and perhaps somewhat more flexible because of the impact of certain postmodern trends; however, in my opinion it does not otherwise change significantly. The key point is that it still follows the basic procedures of grounded theory even if at times the goals vary. In addition, it still interprets the data because Charmaz (2000) has acknowledged that "Constructivist grounded theory spawns an image of a writer at a desk who tries to balance theoretical interpretation with an evocative aesthetic" (p. 526).

**Hermeneutics**. As is well known, hermeneutic procedures began with biblical studies, which met the initial condition for its practice because the Bible's origins and authors were unknown and difficult to determine, if at all. Hermeneutics developed into a philosophy that tried to ascertain the meaning of phenomena whose origins were obscure or ambiguous. The philosophical hermeneutics of Heidegger and Gadamer did not deal with methods so much as with the articulation of being or truth. The philosopher who did take up the issue of hermeneutic method in the tradition of Dilthey was Paul Ricoeur (1981b), who first argued that human behavior could be understood as a text and then showed how hermeneutic methods could be applied to descriptions of human behavior.

However, the hermeneutic researchers we chose did not follow Ricoeur's approach except in the general sense that they employed the hermeneutic circle. Rather, they picked a few ideas from Heidegger's ontological philosophy, incorporated them into the hermeneutic circle, and applied them ontically. I do not know how generic such a method can be and whether ontological understandings can be simply transferred to ontic levels without some type of modification.

The hermeneutic procedure did, however, result in interpretations of human behavior. The hermeneutic method was always practiced within the perspective of the human science tradition even if it initiated *avant la lettre*. The emphasis was always on the expressed meanings of texts and their clarification. But, as with the empirical tradition, what is revealed is usually only the external results of the method. That is, the outcomes of the analyses are communicated but little about the conscious processes involved. The extent to which certain contents are revealed are mostly noematic phrases that were pivotal for the researcher, but not their noetic correlates. We do not know what interpretive suggestions were considered and rejected or why the ones chosen were considered to be the best. We simply know what the final interpretations are but are left in the dark with respect to why they were deemed to be the best. The critic, of course, can go through an interpretive process with the same raw data, but there is no guarantee that he is traversing the same themes that the original investigator considered.

**Phenomenology**. As stated, the view adopted here is that of Husserlian descriptive phenomenology. The major task of this meaning of phenomenology is to describe carefully what is given without presuppositions and then use this concrete description as a basis to methodically determine the essence of that experience. The analysis and results are conducted and expressed within the phenomenological attitude rather than in the natural attitude, the latter attitude being assumed by empiricism and hermeneutics. The scientific interpretation of this project is practically identical to the philosophical one except that certain critical differences are introduced to establish the scientific status of the praxis. For example, psychological phenomenology is identical to philosophical phenomenology in its understanding of intentionality and intuition: The latter term refers to the fact that many acts of consciousness are directed toward objects, and the former term refers to the fact that objects as they are can be "awarefully" present to consciousness. Slightly different criteria for scientific phenomenology are introduced with respect to the type of phenomenological attitude, eideticism, and apriority. Each criterion is respected, but the scientific attitude demands that the phenomenological attitude not be transcendental but psychological (scientific); nevertheless, the objects are understood to be presences but not posited as existing. The eidetic discoveries are described as typical, not universal; however, imaginative variation is still employed, and the categories are understood to be a priori but with a more limited range of inclusion because of the impact of the empirical data. Thus, all of the philosophical criteria are honored, even if certain deviations are introduced to meet scientific standards.

## Evaluation of Philosophical Bases

Since all three qualitative methods are faithful to the philosophies that underlie them, a comparison will be made primarily between philosophies rather than between methods, although implications for the latter will also be mentioned when important. Of course, empiricism has a long and well-established, worthy history. Its many successes cannot be denied; one can only speak of certain limitations. Empiricism's strength lies in the experience of sensorily delineated transcendent objects. Such objects allow for intersubjective scrutiny that usually results in objectively ascertained agreements. As one moves away from such objects empiricism's results begin to waver. Where phenomena resist the effort to be made sensorily public (e.g. the experience of images) indirect procedures are inevitably relied upon. This means that all phenomena immanent to consciousness are accessed only with difficulty. Since many psychological phenomena consist of such immanent data, the empirical approach limits the full development of psychology. It is a robust approach with most transcendent phenomena, but it fails to carry over its success to immanent phenomena.

It should be noted that all three philosophies support methods that actually have an identical task and, while there is some overlap among them, ultimately, the approaches and methods are not identical. It turns out that they are parallel processes, the differences reflecting the different philosophies that support the methods. The identical task may be described as the attempt to come up with a precise disciplinary meaning of data expressed in the language of everyday life. The empirical part is the descriptive data provided by participants. However, the analysis of the data and the disciplinary meanings assigned to such data are as dependent on the theoretical, disciplinary perspective adopted as on the data as such. Hence, it would be better to describe all the methods as empirically based rather than as simply empirical.

For example, we mentioned above that Glaser and Strauss came up with the sociological category "social loss" as the result of their analysis of nurses' responses to dying patients. The actual nurses' responses such as, "He was so young" and "She had a full life," etc., were, according to Glaser and Strauss (1967, p. 106), expressing the sociological idea of "social loss." (One could also say that they intuited the sociological essence of the nurses' everyday expressions, but of course, as empiricists, Glaser and Strauss would not use that language.) They can justify their finding because having adopted a theoretical, sociological attitude they could see that all of the nurses' expressions could be translated into the sociological theoretical term "social loss." But how did they get from "he was so young" etc., to "social loss?" We are told that it is a disciplinary (sociological) insight. But how is the connection made between the raw data Glaser and Strauss analyzed and the insight with which they came up? It is of course extremely plausible—perhaps even completely accurate. But how did it happen? We are given the data and are told, from an external perspective, what the researchers did. They looked at the data, analyzed it, and came up with the insight. But we know nothing about the conscious processes that took place as they analyzed the data. Articulation of the reflection on conscious processes as data are analyzed is not empiricism's strength.

We also must note that the empirical analysis results in a theory, which is the outcome being sought. Such an outcome fits in well with empirical philosophy. Whatever knowledge is initially acquired is always considered tentative until verified and agreed to by others. This is a standard procedure for the empirical perspective.

The hermeneutic approach began with the interpretation of linguistically expressed meanings and has continued to work in that manner. What particularly differentiates it from the empirical approach is that it acknowledges it always begins with a complex, unclear situation that requires the active participation of the researcher in order to achieve a certain degree of clarification. Since the ultimate clarified meaning arrived at requires the activities of the researcher, his or her engagement is essential and so it is committed to an interpretative strategy. There is an acknowledgement that the researcher is too engaged with the experiential process being studied for there to be the "objective-type" judgments that prevail in the natural sciences. Still, the researcher finds that he or she is able to discriminate certain significant meanings in the data that are related to the assumed perspective, which results in the discovery of certain disciplinary meanings by means of which the raw data can be interpreted.

Addison (1989), for example, studied the socialization process of student physicians. He reports that he became immersed in that world and tried to organize his understanding of it. Addison (1989, p. 44) states that over time he "began to see patterns, flows, and directions in their (the residents') behaviors." Why his observations were interpretations rather than descriptions of residents' behaviors is not made clear. In any case, Addison relates that he later began to see what grounded theorists call a "core concept": How did residents experience the first year of residency? Basically, they survived it. So, he saw "survival" as the concept that could tie together the varied experiences that the first-year residents were undergoing. Unlike Glaser and Strauss, Addison took over a term first used by his participants, deciding that the term "survival" basically captured the dynamics of the process that the residents were living. (Again, we could say that

Addison intuited the essence of the residents' first-year experience to be one of survival, but as a hermeneutic researcher he would not use that language). But how did he make that determination? We do not know. Again, it seems plausible, but why? Why did a term used by one or several of his participants appear to Addison to be precisely the notion that would help him understand and articulate the lived experiences of the residents he was studying? Of course, if one cannot justify the use of a term, it is possible to call it an interpretation and move on.

As with the empirical approach, the reviewer of an interpretive analysis is usually only aware of the results of the analysis. The specific application of the method and the choices made by the original researcher are usually not shared with others. Sometimes the process of making a difficult decision is shared with a reader, but a full description of the immanent processing that took place is not forthcoming. Usually, the choice is described in terms of the meanings the raw data provided that formed the basis of the discriminations, not in terms of the noetic processes involved. In addition, the results are understood to be the best interpretation that could be obtained, but often the process by which that determination was made is not spoken to. Just why a designated interpretation is accepted as the best interpretation is frequently not discussed in depth but merely stated. Researchers agree that the outcome of all hermeneutic research is an interpretation, which is different from the establishment of a fact but entirely appropriate where the initial conditions call for a hermeneutic investigation.

While I have been emphasizing certain limitations with respect to interpretive methods, my argument is actually against the universalization of the interpretive methods rather than with their use. There is absolutely nothing wrong with interpretive methods when nothing else can be done. At such times it is a highly respected and necessary procedure. But it is a less desirable substitute for description when descriptions are possible. It is tempting to posit a continuum between descriptive articulation, or explication, and interpretation, but it is necessary to insert a rupture in such a proposed continuum. Description focuses on the given and so is guided by the noematic side of the noesis–noema relationship. It must adhere to the articulation of what is given and explicate it. Interpretation is guided more by noetic factors. Since the given is obscure or not fully present, the conscious acts have to imagine what might have been fully and clearly given, even though it is lacking. These imaginary acts are, of course, guided by the nature of the obscure givens and have to produce types of closure that are harmonious with the partial presences that are perceived. When all is said and done, interpretation is a function of the imagination, and description is a type of perception that follows the articulation of the given.

Descriptive phenomenological psychology is a bit different from the first two procedures in several ways. Because it is descriptive, phenomenology's claim is epistemologically stronger: It says that this is how things present themselves to acts of consciousness. Of course, one can always be wrong, but its stronger claim invites greater criticism and also gives more confidence in findings, with both attitudes helpful for science. Consequently, while grounded theory comes up with theories and hermeneutics results in interpretations, phenomenology's descriptive psychological approach emphasizes presentational findings. Even though the results are expressed in terms of "lived meanings," they have the solidity of facts. The claim is made that the experiences were actually lived in the light of the discovered meanings. The price paid is that only a small segment of an experience is usually so determinedly established. Theories tend to cover larger segments of experience, but precisely because they do so they tend to be more vulnerable. Both approaches have value but they should not be confused with each other.

We also want to make clear why phenomenology can continue with a descriptive method as far as it can. Because phenomenology takes on the challenge of attempting to clarify the immanent processes of consciousness, it has developed a vocabulary for referring to those processes. It speaks of intentionality, constitution, noesis, noema, reduction, immanent, transcendent, and so on. All these terms refer to universal processes, or objects, of consciousness and can be easily verified by simple acts of reflection. For example, intentionality refers to the fact that many acts of consciousness are directed toward objects; a simple act of reflection tells me that I am at the moment aware of my computer, which is transcendent (external) to my consciousness. Or, constitution refers to the fact that acts of consciousness make manifest the phenomena of the world, and I look out my window and see snow. Acts of consciousness were necessary for that perception to occur and thus were constitutive with respect to the appearance of the snow. These terms help us explore the functioning of consciousness, which is necessarily constantly present because it is the medium of access to whatever is given in experience.

The concern for the clarification of immanent processes, as well as the outcomes, is another way that descriptive phenomenology differs from the other two philosophies. When a descriptive researcher approaches the data, he brings with him an immanent framework. As he begins to interrogate the data, he concentrates on the multiple changes that his interrogation brings about. He's aware that his interrogating acts are producing changes in the data and that ultimately his analysis will result in the transformation of some prescientific data into a more clarified psychological understanding. He is constantly present to and assesses such changes.

For example, in a description of learning, a participant writes, "I began to feel uncomfortable with not contributing more to the process of meeting the needs of all of us in the house." The phenomenological researcher reads this sentence with a certain perspective: In the writer's situation, how does this comment contribute to the phenomenon of learning? How can I express what the writer meant in the most psychologically relevant way? To the researcher, the first part of the participants' sentence signifies that all is not going well with the participant. Something is amiss. The second part of the sentence tells the researcher that the participant feels as though she is not contributing sufficiently to the situation she is sharing with others. The researcher wonders if this is a verifiable mood or something the participant is wrongly feeling. Unable to answer that question as yet, the researcher holds the issue in abeyance and proceeds to the next part of the description. But he retains from the analysis so far that perhaps the notion that the participant feels she is not contributing to a group process as well as she could might be contributory to her experience of learning. Of course, the researcher holds on to this notion tentatively until he sees whether or not this idea integrates well with ideas from the other parts of the description. But the point is that the researcher is clear about what he is retaining from the analytic process of that part of the description. What he retains is fully present to his consciousness. It is not an interpretation because the researcher is describing the idea that presented itself to his consciousness as he questioned the participant's account from a disciplinary perspective. It is a description of the possible disciplinary understanding of what the participant said prescientifically.

This process can be described in even greater detail. As the researcher begins to interrogate the raw data, one could say that he is functioning with a vague, anticipated meaning and a missing intentional object (i.e., it is an empty act). For Husserl, meanings are initiated by intentional acts, but in this case, the meaning that is seeking fulfilment is itself specifically unknown and vague, and so what could fulfill it is equally unknown. The researcher is seeking a very specific disciplinary meaning that will essentially capture the contribution to the psychology of learning that this segment of data provides. The researcher is also aware that this is one of the initial steps in the process, so provisional solutions are acceptable at this stage. The process is highly variable and not easily describable. The researcher may try to concentrate on clarifying the meaning so that he can be more certain about what the fulfilling object should look like. Or, the researcher may start varying the original statement by the participant to see if perhaps one of those variations suggests a possible fulfillment that in turn clarifies the meaning to be fulfilled.

More generally, the researcher is seeking a disciplinary meaning for some everyday meanings that the participant expressed in response to a question. The researcher does not know exactly what will satisfy this quest, so he dwells on the vagueness of the task and begins explorations whose goal is the solution of the mini-problem. However, the task is not completely open-ended. There is a criterial framework that must be met: The discovered meaning has to be psychological and fit in coherently with the transformations that are taking place in other parts of the description, etc. Consequently, when the correct phrase comes to mind, the researcher recognizes that it satisfies the mostly non-articulated criteria I have just mentioned. In other words, once the meaning guiding the task has been clarified, the object that appears as its fulfillment is an answer to a specific question posed by the intentional act. Of course, in the critical phase of the analytic process the researcher checks his intuited expression with the relevant criteria. Just how a meaningful intentional act of consciousness produces a sought-for object that fulfills the aim of the empty clarified intentional act is not yet fully understood. But at least the phenomenological analysis has pushed the understanding further than before. The analytic processing of the whole description proceeds in like fashion.

Certain other procedural variations introduced by descriptive phenomenology should also be mentioned. We noted above that grounded theory proceeded by coding and establishing categories and properties. Coding often proceeds by line-by-line analysis (Glaser, 1978, pp. 57–58). There are limitations to both of these procedures. Line-by-line analysis basically allows the physical characteristics of a paper to determine the segments of data to be analyzed. But segments of data determined in such a way may not be the best kind of segment to be analyzed. Even if one is not rigid about the definition of lines, it is still not the best way to establish an analyzable segment of the data. The relationship between an arbitrarily defined line and its meaning is too contingent to be helpful.

In addition, the very process of coding can also be questioned. When one codes, a line or similar segment of data is reduced to a word or a small phrase that is meant to capture its essential meaning. Thus, starting from the very beginning of the analysis we have a reductive procedure. The code word is meant to reactivate all of the associated meanings, but there are usually so many codes that not all of the associated meanings are always reactivated. Consequently, some richness of the data is usually lost.

Because of the phenomenological philosophy upon which it is based, the descriptive method involves different steps in its analysis. Meaning is such a critical part of phenomenological analysis that the method is geared to retain to the extent possible original, spontaneously expressed meanings. Consequently, when the researcher executes the third step of the method (i.e., after assuming the attitude of the phenomenological scientific reduction and reading the entire description for the sense of the whole), he goes through the data and identifies all of the "meaning units" in the description from a psychological perspective and with an attitude of sensitivity to the phenomenon being researched. While distinguishing meaning units is a relative achievement, in the sense that is being done relatively independent of the whole at this stage, it nevertheless retains the meanings as they were initially coherently expressed by the participant in his or her spontaneous context. Since contexts are important for the accurate discrimination of meanings, preserving all of the contexts aids in detecting expressed meanings accurately.

In addition, no coding takes place within descriptive phenomenological psychological analyses. Rather, the entire segment known as a meaning unit is interrogated for its relevance to the purpose of the research. This means that the proximate, explicit, and implicit context of the meaning unit is awakened and explored for the role it plays in the determination of the disciplinary meaning. This process is expansive rather than reductive. More often than not, the articulation of the transformed meaning unit is longer than the original one because relevant implicit contextual features are made explicit. The motive for this step flows from phenomenological philosophy's rule that all parts of the data are presumed to be equally important until analyzed. Only after an analysis has been completed can the relative significance of different parts of the data be assessed.

Finally, it must be mentioned that only phenomenology explicitly deals with meanings as irreal entities. For Husserl (1983), the real consists of objects that are in space and time and are regulated by causality. But Husserl also acknowledges that humans can be present to objects that may lack one of those characteristics, and he considers them irreal. In addition to meanings, numbers, concepts, and syllogisms are also irreal objects for Husserl. Consequently, that is why Husserl spends so much time trying to delineate the immanent processes of consciousness because they are also irreal, and he uses them to account for the presence of irreal objects as well as real ones. Empiricism does not directly acknowledge the existence of irreal entities and tries to account for their presence in numerous indirect ways. While there are hermeneutic thinkers who acknowledge irreal dimensions of the world (e.g., Heidegger), those aspects are rarely discussed by hermeneutic psychological investigators, who tend to stay with the linguistic expressions used by their participants. Moreover, Ricoeur (1981c, pp. 115–116) explicitly argues against both the reduction and an idealistic understanding of meaning for hermeneutics.

By way of summary, it can be said that although the philosophies that support the three qualitative methods (grounded theory, hermeneutics, and descriptive phenomenology) are irreducibly different, they nevertheless support methods that share a single goal and help each method to achieve that goal. The common goal is to express from the perspective of a disciplinary viewpoint the basic disciplinary meaning of everyday expressions used by naive participants in critical situations. Empiricism, via the grounded theory method, relies on the utterances made by participants and uses such utterances as the basis for insights that lead to pertinent disciplinary meanings. Hermeneutic researchers analyze the expressions made by naive participants and probe them until they reveal a deeper, disciplinary meaning. Descriptive phenomenological psychological researchers explore and note the immanent conscious processes the researcher has lived through in order to determine the essential disciplinary meaning lived by the participants. The different phraseologies employed above reflect the different assumptions and perspectives of the three philosophies.

It is also important to note that each method has its own vulnerability. Empiricism via grounded theory results in theories, and such outcomes are less valid than established facts or laws because the theory can be wrong. Hermeneutics results in interpretations, which by definition implies that all other interpretations have not been eliminated; thus, it is possible that another interpretation could prove to be the correct one. Descriptive phenomenology has great confidence in the fact that whatever eidetically presents itself to the consciousness of the researcher is correct; however, there is no guarantee that the phenomenon really exists the way that it presented itself to the researcher.

Finally, it has to be said that lurking behind all of these analyses is the huge and important problem of the meaning of meaning, and all three philosophies differ significantly with respect to that issue. There are several theories of meaning within empiricism, and the hermeneutic understanding of meaning is very different from that of descriptive phenomenology. Attempting to resolve the differences within each philosophy and then across the three philosophical perspectives is an enormous undertaking that is way beyond scope of this paper.

### Notes

[1] I am not sure that Packer still maintains the position he expressed in this book. Since the publication of the book he edited with Addison, Packer (2011) published another book on qualitative research. While he is still hermeneutic and the new book contains traces of the position he advocated in 1989, he has added a whole new perspective based on the work of Foucault. I have decided to stay with the 1989 book because of the diversity of authors and because it is much less ideological than the new book.

[2] I committed myself to the use of Packer and Addison's (1989) book based upon the chapters written by the editors. I simply assumed that the remaining chapters written by the other authors followed, in general, what the authors established about the hermeneutic method. I later read the other chapters in order to see what kinds of variations they might have employed, which is when I detected that except for the chapter by Brown et al. (1989), no other author explicitly used the procedure known as the hermeneutic circle.

[3] I do not believe that every research article necessarily has to reproduce all of the steps actually lived by the researcher as long as the steps actually employed are clear. Not all readers are methodologists who would be interested in the details of the results produced by application of the method. However, there should be an article available that does demonstrate all the details of the application of a method so

that a reader of the original article can refer to that source and at least
have some sense of the methodical process that produced the results
being read.

# Chapter 2

## Further Reflections on the Roles of Description and Interpretation in Phenomenological Qualitative Methods

Recently, Rennie (2012) tried to make the claim that the scientific descriptive phenomenological method that I developed based upon the thought of Edmund Husserl (1983) and Maurice Merleau-Ponty (1962) was an interpretive method despite the explicitly opposite claim of its title. Without explicitly acknowledging it, Rennie was advocating the position known as hermeneutic universalism (Shusterman, 1991), which holds that all meaningful experiences are the result of interpretation. I (Giorgi, 2014) responded with a critique of Rennie's position and arguments and made a distinction between conducting a research project, which I admitted was interpretive, and the method employed, which I claimed could still be descriptive (although interpretive methods are equally possible). In arguing for the descriptive approach, I recognized the importance of predication for the descriptive method. In this article, I want to delve more deeply into the question of predication and its role in description, as well as how it differs from linguistic expressions that are called interpretations.

My position is that both interpretation and description are legitimate linguistic functions but that they take place under different conditions. In general, neither one nor the other should be eliminated from qualitative research. The effort to reduce either one to the other is fallacious, and the effort to use only one process can be severely limiting. Briefly, description is the use of language to articulate the intentional objects of experience with the claim that the linguistic expression accurately articulates the non-linguistic state of affairs or object to which it refers. Of course, one can be wrong, but the claim is made nonetheless. This type of expression is often referred to as a predication. Interpretation is the use of language to articulate the most plausible meaning of a state of affairs or object, but it lacks a definitive claim. This is because other equally plausible meanings could not be eliminated or because the supporting evidence for the chosen interpretation lacked conclusiveness. The issues surrounding this distinction will be discussed further, but the contrast above is offered as an initial guide.

There is a rather pervasive use of description in science. In the history of psychology, the idea that psychology should be at least in part a descriptive science has been suggested many times (Brentano, 1973; Dilthey, 1977; Politzer, 1968). And even if it was understood that psychology should not be completely descriptive, descriptions were in constant use in research and other practices (Titchener, 1901a; 1901b; Freud, 1900; Piaget, 1932; Simon and Ericsson, 1980). In addition, the apparatus and procedure sections of every research report contain descriptions of the equipment and procedures used, if only so that replications of the original studies could be conducted. Finally, clinical case studies contain descriptions of the clients' symptoms as well as of the interpretations that the clinicians provided.

Interpretations also abound in the scientific world. One could say that every theory offered to explain certain phenomena is an interpretation of worldly events that have taken place. The same is true of provisionary clinical understandings of client abnormalities. The cautionary approach of science in general motivates scientists to move slowly so that tentative explanations are initially offered rather than conclusive ones; such a procedure supports an interpretive approach. Thus, there are strong motives for interpretations in science.

Since the advent of the interpretive turn in science during the latter part of the last century, a position known as hermeneutic universalism has reached a kind of ascendancy. If one accepts such a position, it means that descriptions would no longer be possible. All linguistic expressions would become interpretations, with the consequence that all statements would be plausible but not definitive. However, not all those who espouse a hermeneutic perspective accept that it is universalist. I will demonstrate this point by quoting two leading hermeneutic theorists who acknowledge non-interpretive expressions. For example, Taylor (1985) has written:

> Interpretation, in the sense relevant to hermeneutics, is an attempt to make clear, to make sense of, an object of study. The object must, therefore, be a text, or a text-analogue, which in some way is confused, incomplete, cloudy, seemingly

contradictory—in one way or another, unclear. The interpretation aims to bring to light an underlying coherence or sense. (p. 150)

One could say that Taylor is describing (i.e., making a definitive claim) the condition that must be met in order for an expression or a phenomenon to motivate an interpretive effort. If clarity or transparency is present, interpretation is not called for. Gadamer (1979) made this point directly when he wrote:

We speak of interpretation when the meaning of a text is not understood at first sight; then an interpretation is necessary. In other words, an explicit reflection is required on the conditions that enable the text to have one or another meaning. The first presupposition that implies the concept of interpretation is the "foreign" character of what is yet to be understood. Indeed, whatever is immediately evident, whatever persuades us by its simple presence, does not call for any interpretation. (p. 90)

Gadamer is affirming that there are expressions or events that are transparent in their appearance and therefore do not call for interpretations. Such events or phenomena can be described. Finally, Shusterman (1991) has advanced several powerful arguments against the thesis of hermeneutic universalism, which we shall refer to below. Scientists have to cope with different forms of expression. The constant usage of both types of these linguistic expressions (descriptions and interpretations) requires us to look into each of them more closely.

**Description and Predication**: I have asserted that description is the use of language to articulate the intentional objects of experience. But there is more. The articulation also carries with it the claim that it accurately reflects the non-linguistic state of affairs or object, at least thematically so. One could also say that descriptions contain multiple predications. But what is a predication? Webster's dictionary states that with predication "something...is affirmed or denied of the subject in a proposition in logic." Also, according to Webster, predication means "to proclaim publicly, to assert, to affirm, to declare," and finally, "to found, base, as in, his theory is predicated on recent findings." All of these expressions communicate the sense that something "is." In predication there is an assertion that an object or state of affairs exists or presents itself precisely in the way that the linguistic expression declares it to be.

Husserl (1973) has provided a description of the process of predication, and it is the basis of what follows. Husserl's overall motivation in Experience and Judgment was to work out a genealogy of logic, so he tackled a number of intricate problems related to that theme in that work. However, I will concentrate specifically on the phenomenon of predication. Abstractly put, Husserl (1973) described the overall predicative sequence in general as follows: There is a prepredicative experience, which includes an implicit awareness; then the act of predication itself, with the production of a categorial object; then the maintaining or holding-in-grasp of the categorial object, the role of will and ego; and, finally, the production of sense. I shall now discuss this process a bit more. In doing so, I will also draw from important articles by Moneta (1972) and Gurwitsch (1973).

Husserl (1973) notes that an act of predication is rooted in prepredicative experiences. Prepredicative experiences are essentially perceptual and refer to the self-givenness of objects and states of affairs and their modes of self-givenness. It should be recalled that perceptual experiences take place within a structure that includes the horizon of the world, which is not an explicit awareness, but rather a type of implicit awareness that reveals the role of belief that accompanies such a consciousness. As Moneta (1972) says:

> The being-there of the world is passively accepted and endorsed by consciousness. This acceptance is not articulated in any explicit act of consciousness; it rather constitutes an unreflective state whose intentional character is that of belief-in a world within which consciousness finds itself. (p. 173)

So, it is already at the prepredicative level that we discover the horizon structure of consciousness and its obscurity. It is also at this level that we discover a distinction between the object of experience and the mode in which it is given. For Husserl, the mode of givenness "plays a constitutive role in the formation of the predicative judgment" (Moneta, 1972, p. 174). Indeed, "self-givenness and the mode of this self-givenness constitute the primary structures of prepredicative experience" (Moneta, 1972, p. 174).

At this prepredicative level, one also encounters the implicit awareness of the horizon of experience, especially the world horizon within the context of which every given occurs. One also encounters the natural attitude that highlights the "belief-in" of the world and all its objects. All of this is actually preparatory for the act of predication. As

Husserl (1973) says, "Every judging presupposes that an object is on hand, that it is already given to us, and is that about which the statement is made" (p. 14). But the structure of the experience at prepredicative levels is constituted passively, and it is not yet a field of true objects. Husserl nevertheless notes that "this field is still not a pure chaos, a mere 'swarm' of 'data'; it is a field of determinate structure, one of prominences and articulated particularities" (p. 72). And the horizon of this experience is more lived than known.

After this phase, predication proper can emerge. Since, as Zaner (1972) forcefully asserts, for Husserl,

> the fundamental aim of phenomenology (the discipline of criticism) is the search for, and the discovery and the faithful articulation of, 'lasting cognitive possessions'—that is, knowledge as a corpus of eidetic insights systematically connected with other eidetic insights which as 'science' are necessarily sharable with other critical philosophers and theorists, (p. 224)

the aim of predication is to determine once and for all the sense of the object. The movement is carried out by a process Husserl calls "contemplative perception" or, as Gurwitsch (1973) calls it, "explicating contemplation" (p. 77). As stated, the process begins passively, but then with an effort of concentration the more passive "looking at" becomes a full seeing of the object; thus, ultimately, a categorial object, "this is P," is formed (Moneta, 1972, p. 178). As Moneta states, "In the unfolding of the contemplative process there occurs an alteration of the originary object sense," so "the perceived object has thus acquired a new sense, the predicable sense." It is by "holding-in-grasp' or "maintaining-in-grasp" that the properties to be explicated become detected (p. 179). Moneta summarizes the process as follows:

> This new sense is neither derived from the passive domain nor from any other level of consciousness's activity, but it has been "produced" by the specific activity of predication. It is in virtue of this "productive" character of consciousness's activity that we have risen to the cognitive level of experience in the pregnant sense. (p. 180)

Consequently, a new sense, a predicative statement, emerges, and that activity requires the appearance of the ego and the will, new dimensions not present in the prepredicative phase. Since predication operates at the level of cognitive consciousness, it involves the ego, which has the will to establish the "once-for-all determination" of the object of consciousness. This can happen because consciousness also has the ability to "hold-in-grasp" the object under review.

Gurwitsch (1973) goes along with Husserl's description of the predication process up to a point, but he complements and modifies it. Gurwitsch states that Husserl described the process basically from a noetic perspective, whereas Gurwitsch wants to emphasize the noematic aspects that he believes corrected some weak points in Husserl's account. Because of his noetic emphasis, Husserl describes the activity of explicating contemplation in terms of an empty substrate to which attributes (e.g., "p" and "q") are attached through synthetic activity while maintaining the substrate in grasp.

On the other hand, Gurwitsch (1973, pp. 82–85) accounts for the noematic structure in terms of organization by Gestalt coherence, where the noematic structure is a differentiated unity in which the internoematic system as such is contained in each of its attributes—a matter of coherence rather than one of inherence in Husserl's account, whereby each attribute inheres in a substratum. Despite differences in the description of the process of predication because of different noetic and noematic emphases, Gurwitsch (1973) concurs with Husserl with respect to the conclusion of the process when he states,

> Articulating thematization proves to be a special mental operation performed upon a given perceptual situation which hereby undergoes categorial formation. To that specific operation corresponds a specific noematic correlate, namely the state of affairs (Sachverhalt) which is the *judgmental noema* founded upon, but different from, the perceptual noema. (p. 84, itallics in original)

We are not so much interested in following all the intricacies of the predicative process as in identifying the role of description in that process. Throughout the entire analysis of predication, the term "interpretation" is never used. Husserl always spoke of describing the process of predication and, in each step of the process described his findings as did Moneta and Gurwitsch. If Husserl believed that it was description that was called for in these analyses, it is because of his philosophical phenomenological stance. In speaking of descriptions within the natural attitude, Husserl (2006) wrote:

Of course, when I describe what is experienced or simply found I make judgments. But these purely descriptive judgments are, as such, mere expressions of the experiences, of what has been found, and are, as such, in a certain sense absolutely evident, namely, evident precisely as mere expressions, just as the description of a fiction, if it is faithful, clearly has this evidence. If the I describes that which is found or experienced in its particular determinateness or indefinite generality, then all this is posited as being, and, notwithstanding the evidence belonging to the correctness of the expression, which may be a perfect one, the judgment comes with the evidence of the thesis of experience, which, to be sure, is an evidence, but, speaking generally, is an imperfect evidence nevertheless. Everyone knows that "experience can deceive." Everyone knows, indeed, everyone has the right, upon pursuing the evidence, to assert what is experienced. Nevertheless, everyone knows that what is experienced "may not really be the case." (pp. 10–11)

So Husserl is affirming the validity of descriptions of experiences in the natural attitude up to a point. The descriptions have to be taken seriously, but the positing that also takes place within the natural attitude has to be critically evaluated. Husserl's analysis indicates what part of a description can be trusted and what part is not trustworthy; it is positing the existing of what is described that could be mistaken. Husserl (2006) continues his analysis of the extent to which validity can be ascribed to descriptions within the natural attitude by saying:

And it is further evident that my judgments, provided that they, as we set them up, are pure expressions of the perceived as such, of the remembered as such, etc., will exclude any possible error, because they reflect then in the pure descriptive expressions the mere sense of the particular perceptions, memories, other experiential certitudes, etc. It may well be the case that I am deceived in thinking that the thing is there, but that I perceive, and that the perception is of a thing with a spatial surrounding, etc., that is indubitable.... The general expressions, with which I...describe perception, memory, etc., as perception as such, memory as such, and correspondingly...the universal expressions which I use, in regard to what is perceived as such, etc., as when I speak of persons and things, etc. .... Signify a general sense to which any empirical truth is clearly bound. It may well be that occasionally I am deceived in believing that an object I think is vis-à-vis me is indeed there or exists in such a fashion as it appears to me. But it does appear, and before I entertain the question whether it truly is and how it is in reality, I know from the very outset that it can only be in accordance to *the* sense in which a thing with properties, etc., exists—for it is as this that it appears perceptually. (pp. 22–23, itallics in original)

One could say that within the natural attitude there is the thing itself that appears and the sense and mode with which it appears. Husserl is asserting that the sense (it appears as a chair) and the mode (it is perceived) cannot be doubted. But whether the object itself really is as it appears to be has to be ascertained by other means, and it could be other than what it appeared to be (it could be a fake chair or some kind of chair analogue that appears as a chair.)

In the phenomenological attitude, Husserl insists, one does not make judgments about the positing of the existence of the object that is perceived; rather, one concentrates on the sense and mode of the given. I am certain that it is a perceived chair that my experience has presented to me, so my epistemological claim relates to what has been experientially given and not to the existence of the given. The latter may not exist precisely in the manner in which the appearance that I had suggested should be, but whatever does exist has to be harmonious with the sense of the appearance. In other words, what exists cannot be an amorphous blob of matter but has to be something that is at least an analogue of a chair—e.g., a projection of a chair on a screen that I took to be real. The actual existing object has to in some sense suggest "chairness."

Thus, within the phenomenological attitude, and to be genuinely phenomenological all research has to take place within that attitude, one can now understand why description is called for. It's because the presentations cannot be doubted; one is dealing with the very initial presences to consciousness, not empirical realities. This means that these noemata are transparent and convincingly present and so call for descriptions. The sense of the experiences meet the condition for description.

We now come to a controversial point: Which is more basic, description or interpretation? I have heard both sides of the issue: that interpretation is basic and that description is a special type of interpretation, and that description is primary and that interpretation is a special kind of description. I think that the latter position is the true one and for this reason: It has been repeatedly emphasized that it is not only the object that appears that is important but also the mode of givenness of the object. Husserl (1983, pp. 249–257) speaks of the doxic characteristics (belief-characteristics) noetically and of existential characteristics (being characteristics) noematically. Husserl (1983) puts it as follows:

> As noetic characteristics related to correlative modes of being—"doxic" or "belief characteristics"—we find perceptual belief and, sometimes, to be sure, perceptual certainty, really inherently included in intuitive objectivations, e.g., in those of normal perceptions as "attentive perceptions"; corresponding to <perceptual certainty> as its noematic correlate belonging to the appearing object is the being-characteristic "actual". In the sphere considered up to now, that which appears perceptually or memorially had the characteristic of "actually" existing simpliciter—of "certainly" existing as we also say in contrast to other being-characteristics....the mode of *"certain" belief* can change into the mode of mere *deeming possible* or *deeming likely*, or *questioning* and *doubting*; and, as the case may be, that which appears....has taken on now the *being-modalities* of *"possible,"* of *"probable,"* of *"questionable,"* of *"doubtful."* (pp. 249–250; italics in original)

Consequently, when Husserl speaks of the sense and mode that cannot be doubted, he is speaking of those situations where the acts and objects (or noeses and noemata) present themselves precisely in that way. But since Husserl admits that there are modalities other than certitude within which objects can present themselves, and since we know that interpretation calls precisely for presentations that are problematic or ambiguous in some fashion, this means that the condition for interpretation can be recognized and described. That is, one can describe exactly the manner in which the presentation is ambiguous or unclear. Therefore, it seems that a descriptive orientation is more fundamental for research because it allows for description when that condition is present (clarity), and it can also describe the condition that calls for interpretation (unclarity).     In other words, regardless of the mode of givenness of the object or state of affairs, a descriptive orientation can continue to function, whereas someone in an interpretive mode when confronted with a clear object finds that there is no task to be done. A hermeneutic researcher not espousing hermeneutic universalism would presumably be able to switch to descriptive mode. While a descriptivist could move to an interpretive mode, he or she could also remain in the descriptive attitude and carefully describe the nature of the ambiguity or the unclarity of the given. Such a careful description might even suggest a way out of the difficulty. In any case, a descriptivist would not necessarily have to resort to interpretation. An interpretive researcher encountering a clear object would find interpretive activity to be superfluous or simply an arbitrary exercise.

## A Critique of Hermeneutic Universalism

I hope that it is clear by now that I affirm that a hermeneutic method is a legitimate way of conducting research in the human sciences. In fact, one might say that it is the most predominant manner of doing research if one interprets the hypothetical-deductive method as a hermeneutic one in the sense that the hypothesis could be considered as a tentative interpretation that is subsequently supported or denied by the gathering of empirical data. Authors who have argued for a hermeneutic approach for research include Gadamer (1975), although not specifically for hermeneutic methods for the human sciences; Taylor (1985); Ricoeur (1981); Radnitsky (1970); and the authors included in the edited book by Packer and Addison (1989), wherein a variety of methods are in display. My one objection is to the thesis of hermeneutic universalism, which claims that hermeneutics is the only method of research for the human sciences.

It is important to note that some scholars who foster the hermeneutic method nevertheless resist espousing hermeneutic universalism. Shusterman (1991) is such a scholar and has enumerated several reasons why the hermeneutic universalistic thesis should not be upheld. First of all, Shusterman (1991, pp.108–119) connects the thesis of hermeneutic universalism with the rejection of foundationalism. Since interpretations are generally regarded as being corrigible, perspectival, prejudiced, and the result of active mental processes, once foundationalism—the idea of a transparent, absolute and univocal truth—is rejected, then the inference is quickly made by some hermeneutic thinkers that all knowledge is interpretive. However, Shusterman believes that such an inference still retains vestiges of foundationalism because it assumes that there can be absolute understandings and therefore refuses to acknowledge that understandings can be corrigible, perspectival, and prejudiced without necessarily being interpretive. He argues that once foundationalism is truly surpassed then it is permissible to allow for understandings, derived in non-interpretive ways, to have the characteristics of the type of knowledge that interpretations have. The difference then turns on the manner in which the knowledge is obtained. Shusterman (1991) speaks to this difference as follows:

> While understanding, even intelligent understanding, is often unreflective, unthinking, indeed unconscious (even if always purposive), interpretation proper involves conscious, deliberate thought: a clarification of something obscure or ambiguous, a deciphering of a symbol, an unraveling of a paradox, an articulation of previously unstated formal or semantic relations between elements....interpretation characteristically involves a problem-situation. (p. 126)

In the above statement, we see Shusterman basically confirming the conditions under which interpretations take place. However, he also admits that non-interpretive understandings can occur but does not explicitly state, as we do, that such understandings should be described. He also perhaps limits the type of understandings that call for description. There can be a deepening of a presented meaning that calls for descriptive articulation rather than interpretation. Descriptive phenomenologists and interpretive phenomenologists differ on this point, but at least it should be mentioned that there is a descriptive response to the usual claim that the uncovering of deep meanings is always interpretive. Mohanty (1987) has written:

> In so far as the method suggested by Heidegger does not confine itself to what is *prima facie* given, to what is obvious, but tries to uncover what is hidden and implicit, the methodological program still conforms to the descriptive ideal. In the second place, some of these deep phenomena are themselves interpretations or meanings conferred by man in the course of his historical existence, on himself and on his world; and it may be that human existence is meaning-conferring and interpreting. If that is so, then interpretations, insofar as they

are uncovered, are themselves phenomena and are amenable to description.... That description uncovers interpretations which are immanent to the phenomenon being described does not alter the fact that what is being done is description. (p. 57, itallics in original)

The difference may be subtle, but if during the unfolding of a complex meaning what presents itself is clear after critical evaluation, then the condition for description has been met. In other words, complexity in and of itself is not a criterion for interpretation. If in the process of unfolding a complex meaning certain distinctions and discriminations are made, and judgments about what is more or less important are decided, all of those activities can still fall under the head of description if a certain degree of clarity persists. What matters is whether there is a given that is easily and quickly apprehended or a gap. If the former, then the condition for description still prevails; if the latter, then the condition for interpretation is met. The length or complexity of the process is not a criterion for distinguishing between the two procedures.

Bohman (1991) accepts a hermeneutic perspective, but within that perspective he distinguishes between a strong holistic stance and a weak holistic stance and opts for the latter. While both perspectives are aligned with hermeneutic universalism, the former stance, according to Bohman (1991, p. 134) would "argue that correctness may not be the proper goal of interpretive procedures at all"...which would lead to "the unwarranted skeptical conclusion that valid interpretations do not constitute knowledge based on evidence." He then goes on to identify two premises that the two perspectives share:

Both premises can be read as presenting fundamental conditions for the possibility of interpretation: its circularity and hence its necessary reference to other interpretations; and its assumption of an unanalyzable background, or the necessary presupposition of an indefinite set of other beliefs and practices. (1991, p. 134)

Because of those two conditions—circularity and unanalyzable backgrounds—Bohman states that strong holists argue for contextualism, the notion that interpretations are valid only for their contexts. However, for his own position, that of weak holism, Bohman (1991, 135) maintains that he uses the "same premises to establish a transcendental analysis of interpretation and its own public warrants for correctness." In other words, the perspective of weak holism affirms that certain defensible knowledge claims can be made from an interpretive perspective. In any case, Bohman is a hermeneutic thinker who defends a position regarding knowledge claims that is different from the extreme consequences that most hermeneutic universalists would posit. Thus, while maintaining a hermeneutic perspective, Bohman wants to demonstrate that a type of secure knowledge, such as a descriptive approach offers, can be obtained with hermeneutic analyses.

These authors show that hermeneutic universalism with its contextual knowledge claims is a disputed position among hermeneutic thinkers themselves. Shusterman affirms that reliable knowledge can be obtained in non-interpretive ways, and Bohman claims that a weak holistic perspective can produce defensible knowledge claims, which is what a descriptive orientation wants to claim.

The response of the universalist hermeneut to these objections is to problematize the transparent or clear understanding; this is usually done by referring to the historical or developmental conditions that helped produce the understanding. Thus, if I say, "Today it is raining outside," the obviousness and clarity of that statement has to be rendered dubious. One way would be simply to claim that the very use of language is an interpretive act because the experience is reduced to a limited expression, so it shows that a certain selectivity has taken place and other selections could be possible. Or one could say that all current understandings are based upon past interpretations and so really are interpretations. But such theories do not take into account the concrete, immediate experience of understanding. If we are to have a legitimate experiential science, then all types of experiences have to be understood as they are encountered. As Shusterman (1991) states it:

> Even if these direct or immediate understandings are always based on the founded habits and capacities of prior efforts of interpretation, there is still a difference between such effortless, unthinking acts of understanding (or experiences of meaning) and acts of interpretation, which call for deliberate, focused thought. In marking a difference between interpretation and the direct experiences or understandings on which it is based, ordinary language respects the role of the unformulabe, prereflective, and non-discursive background from which the

foreground of conscious thinking emerges and without which it could never arise. (pp. 123–124)

In other words, Shusterman is appealing to the criteria we have been using in distinguishing interpretation from the conditions for description. If something is transparent, however it may have developed, interpretation is simply not necessary, and there are such experiences.

## The Hermeneutic Perspective

I want to acknowledge that there is no doubt in my mind that solid science can be conducted from an interpretive perspective. In fact, as mentioned above, if we understand science in a large sense, so that we can conceive of the hypothetic-deductive method as an interpretive strategy, then most of science is conducted interpretively. The hypothesis that guides particular research may come from theories, assumptions, guesses, or what not, but they can all be considered as plausible interpretations of the phenomenon being studied. Statements that are called theories or assumptions are so called precisely because they do not carry with them the sense that they are incontrovertibly established. When they are secured as established knowledge, they become laws or facts. Consequently, most of science is conducted in terms of theories, hypotheses, and assumptions, or in terms of plausible interpretations about phenomena, because laws and sustaining facts are hard to establish. Nothing that I have said here should surprise any working scientist, although some more conservative scholars might object to being seen as interpretive strategists.

If I continue to maintain the difference between description and interpretation it is because of the difference in the knowledge claims offered by the two perspectives, although Bohman's weak holism partially addresses this issue. But also because it is faithful to the way certain experiences happen. A description carries with it the claim that the articulated expression accurately conveys what was given to the experiencer. Even "best interpretations" must stay within the realm of plausibility. However, I do concede that there are circumstances that may not allow descriptions to be carried out, so one must resort to interpretive strategies. The main circumstances in which descriptions are not possible are those in which the given is missing altogether or else only minimally present. That is because the primary requirement of description is a discipline that requires one to be faithful to the given.

It is wholly object or noema dominated. Interpretation, on the other hand is guided by noetic concerns. Since the object of study is missing or murky, the acts must try to ascertain plausible substitute presences and must somehow make up for what the given lacks. Obviously, imagination plays a role here as well as whatever background knowledge is available to the researcher. Thus, the difference between noetic and noematic emphases is another way of differentiating between interpretation and description.

Yet another way to highlight the difference between the two perspectives is to note, at least with phenomenological descriptions, that an internal perspective to the process is required. If one simply took an external perspective toward the results of a methodical phenomenological descriptive analysis, they would appear to be the same as interpretation. Thus, Rennie (2012), observing the workings of my method from an external perspective, wrote, (incidentally, quite incorrectly with respect to the process): "After all, changing the original text into pithier language and transforming that rewriting into psychological language are patently interpretive moves...." (p. 393). This judgment is based on results and ignores the process by which the changes were made.

However, phenomenological analyses are reflective analyses requiring that one correlate the acts and objects that are functioning within an experience. But since the analysis has to be done within the attitude of the phenomenological reduction, we are correlating noeses and noemata instead of the acts and objects of the natural attitude. If I am analyzing a description from a person from a Lifeworld perspective and want to understand it psychologically, I approach the description from a psychological perspective and begin to seek meanings in the Lifeworld description that are psychologically revealing. Then I begin the task of trying to express the psychological meanings more explicitly—more in line with the purposes of the research. At the beginning of the process I have merely a signifying, empty intention: I see a phrase in the original description that is replete with psychological significance, so I begin looking for an expression that will more adequately highlight the psychological aspect of that part of the description. I am guided by a vague sense that needs to be explored and fulfilled. With the help of free imaginative variation. I come up with several fulfilling attempts and immediately recognize that they are not adequate. Finally, perhaps after several partial fulfillments, I hit upon the perfect expression—the identifying fulfillment.

The identifying fulfillment, which satisfies the signifying intention that initiated the process, is something that presents itself to my consciousness and becomes a given that must be described. This is the only way it can be communicated to a community of researchers. The fact that I am about to present a psychological understanding of an everyday event means that I am making a psychological interpretation of that event, but I am doing so by employing a descriptive method. The project is an interpretive one but the method is descriptive. The project meets the condition for interpretation because the psychological meaning of the Lifeworld description is not transparent. One has to work on the description in order to draw out its psychological meaning. However, the method used meets the condition for description. The researcher has to describe the identifying meanings that present themselves to his consciousness once the psychological labor has been done and must describe them in terms of the modality in which they appear—certainly, probably, doubtfully, etc.

This article has been concerned with the complementary functions of description and interpretation, or straightforward descriptions and interpretive descriptions. The former can be identified with predications—i.e., assertions that carry with them the claim that the state of affairs or objects referred to are exactly the way they were described to be. There are many facts and immediately clear understandings that can be articulated within such a context. Descriptions are dependent on the fact that something is given to consciousness that can be articulated by means of linguistic expressions—and sometimes even with other modes of expression. Within a phenomenological framework, it is the intentional relationship that provides the primary data with its act-object or noesis-noema structure. Even complex givens can be described since the process of unfolding diverse meanings, judging more important and less important meanings, or detecting ambiguous meanings still depends upon something being given. Of course, the sheer fact that something is given does not eliminate the possibility of interpretation, but a scientist following descriptive criteria will refrain from doing so. If there is no given, then interpretation is the more likely strategy to employ.

Interpretation is a descriptive effort that tries to come up with the most plausible understanding of an unclear or problem situation. As stated at the beginning, the outcome is often merely plausible because other possible understandings cannot be eliminated, or else it is clear that the selected understanding is not convincingly conclusive.

Because of the complexity of the world's phenomena, researchers often have to remain content with interpretive results. Such efforts are perfectly legitimate. and good interpretations often suggest other approaches that might provide surer solutions to significant problems. Description and interpretation offer different strengths to scientific researchers, and each should be considered depending upon the circumstances encountered in the course of research.

# Chapter 3

## Concerning Psychological Research on Oneself

Once qualitative methods began to make some headway within the discipline of psychology, it was not long before phenomenological approaches also began to make their impact. However, the variety of approaches that characterized qualitative research in general also spread into phenomenological ways of doing qualitative research. It is not surprising that at the beginning of a movement there are different interpretations of what a correct procedure is. In general, my approach has been to let all of these varieties of methods exist in order to see how well they function and how well they withstand criticism. My special concern is with the quality of phenomenological methods that are applied to psychology because I believe that phenomenology's basic philosophy, especially as articulated by its founder, Husserl, is more than adequate to provide psychology with all that it needs to be an authentic human science.

Among those who founded and articulated a phenomenological method was Clark Moustakas.[1] Before he turned to phenomenology, Moustakas was conducting qualitative research because he claimed to have been using a heuristic method since 1961 (Moustakas, 1990, p. 9) when he explored the phenomenon of loneliness. Moustakas later developed a phenomenological method with insights from Husserlian phenomenological philosophy. Moustakas is the author of both of these attempts to establish a qualitative method, an earlier heuristic method and later a practice he called a phenomenological method. Thus, it is important to see to what extent the heuristic method was guided by phenomenological criteria, even if implicitly so, and if not, to see to what extent some of the steps of the former method might have persevered in his later formulation. The aim here is to see if Moustakas's phenomenological method genuinely reflects phenomenological criteria. This clarification is important because I do believe that the phenomenological method might be useful in researching one's own lived experiences, depending, of course, on how it is implemented.

## The Origins and the Context of the Heuristic Method

Here is what Moustakas (1990) says about what the heuristic method means and the process of discovery experienced by the investigator:

> The root meaning of the word *heuristic* comes from the Greek word *heuriskein*, meaning to discover or to find. It refers to a process of internal search through which one discovers the nature and meaning of experience and develops methods and procedures for further investigation and analysis. The self of the researcher is present throughout the process and, while understanding the phenomenon with increasing depth, the researcher also experiences growing self-awareness and self-knowledge. Heuristic processes incorporate creative self-processes and self-discoveries....The process of discovery leads investigators to new images and meanings regarding human phenomena, but also to realizations relevant to their own experiences and lives. (p. 9; italics in original)

Now, strictly speaking, if heuristic means "to discover or find," then any research project, including quantitative studies, can be called "heuristic." But, clearly, Moustakas does not intend such a universal meaning for the term. He states that the heuristic method is "An organized and systematic form for investigating human experience" (1990, p. 9). Primarily, it is a way of interrogating first-person experiences, often produced by the researcher but also as provided by others. Heuristic research is a way of exploring topics related to personal growth, therapy, creativity, self-actualizing, self-disclosure, and other very personal phenomena. It demands careful description of experiential phenomena followed by detailed reflections on what has taken place.

Heuristic research was launched by Moustakas (1961) with his study of loneliness. If one looks at the book today, one finds not a word about method. Rather it begins with Moustakas's descriptions, sometimes very moving, of his own experience of loneliness, which leads him to wonder about the very phenomenon of loneliness itself. Why is loneliness a phenomenon that humans experience? Can it be avoided? Should it be avoided? If one must suffer through it, is there a deeper lesson about life that can be gleaned from it? What is its real meaning and how does it enlighten human existence? Through careful description and reflections on his own experience, Moustakas tried to answer those and similar questions. He then turned to experiences of loneliness described by others in biographies and journals to see how such accounts could help him deepen his understanding of the phenomenon. Always, it was a matter of personal descriptions and then selective reflection on what he considered to be significant aspects of the description.

Moustakas (1968) writes that his way to the discovery of the heuristic method began with his concern with another problem—the existential crisis he was facing regarding a decision he (and his wife) had to make regarding heart surgery for his young daughter. The problem was that without surgery she would not survive. However, it also was possible that she might not survive the surgical procedure. In the process of attempting to resolve his crisis, Moustakas became aware that he was desperately lonely while trying to formulate a solution to his dilemma. Because of his own concrete experience, he became curious about the phenomenon of loneliness and desired to understand it more thoroughly. His self-observation of being isolated with his lonely feelings seemed to match what he observed with respect to the loneliness of hospitalized children. He writes: "I began to see how young children separated from their parents could often be more completely involved in the struggle with loneliness than in the painful experiences connected with illness and surgery" (p. 106). The discovery that this intriguing phenomenon occurred as much with others as with himself simply whet his appetite to study it more completely.

Moustakas (1968) modestly states that at the beginning his "study of loneliness had no design or purpose, no object or end, and no hypotheses or assumptions" (p. 104). Moustakas undoubtedly means that he had no standard or conventional methodical criteria in mind. However, during the course of his study Moustakas's values changed. Whatever his feelings at the beginning, a purpose did evolve for his research for he says, "Thus I set out to discover the meaning of loneliness in its simplest terms…" (p. 108). A design also emerged because Moustakas also wrote that he desired "to perceive the experience of being lonely in its absolutely native state," and so "set out to discover the nature of lonely experience by intimate encounters…." (p. 108). Again, an end for his research did announce itself because Moustakas wrote, "I decided…to try to understand loneliness, how it fitted into the perceptions and behavior of hospitalized children, and the way in which it existed in myself and others" (p. 107). In the process of conducting his research, assumptions and hypotheses also emerged because Moustakas also stated, "My way of studying loneliness, in its essential form, was to put myself into an open, ready state, into the lonely experiences of hospitalized children, and to let these experiences become the focus of my world" (p. 108). Thus, he assumed that putting himself in an open, ready state would reveal something about loneliness, and he hypothesized, or assumed, that if loneliness became the focus of his world, he would have genuine access to the experience. He also assumed or hypothesized that loneliness had an essential form. Consequently, what differentiates the heuristic method from other modes of conducting experiential research is not the general research criteria, which are common, but the timing of their identification and the manner of defining them.

Moustakas's choice was to stay as close as possible to the stream of experiencing a phenomenon and to describe it in depth, fully and richly. At the beginning, his sole purpose seemed to be to have his own deeply personal experience of loneliness, whether willed or not, so that he could probe and explore it. Subsequently, he sought to become acquainted with the experience of loneliness in others. But apparently, getting to understand a lonely experience was not easy. Moustakas (1968) wrote:

> At the same time, I know from my own experiences....that loneliness could not be communicated by words or defined in its essence, that loneliness could not be known except by persons who are open to their own senses and aware of their own experiences. I set out to discover the nature of lonely experience by intimate encounter with other persons. (p. 108)

Thus, it seems that for the heuristic approach to be successful, concrete episodes of experiencing the phenomenon by the researcher and others are necessary, but somehow the sheer presence of the phenomenon is not sufficient. Some kind of intimate encounter with others, or oneself, is also required, although the nature of that requirement is not specified. Also, which is tricky, Moustakas says that only an experiencer of the phenomenon, who has deep sensitivity and special experiential presence, can know the phenomenon. The qualities that Moustakas assigns to the phenomenon, and to the experiencer of it, make it almost impossible for it to be researched. Given all of these restrictions, one wonders how Moustakas was able to write a book about loneliness.

In order to discover what type of intimate encounter is called for, and what its nature is, I looked for some further clarifications in Moustakas's writings. Some half dozen years later Moustakas (1968) reflected on his initial study of loneliness and for the first time described his procedure for that particular study.[2] I shall repeat his methodical criteria in shortened form. Here's what Moustakas (p. 112) said about "the condition and factors that initiated and characterized the study:

1. A crisis which created a problem
2. A search of self in solitude, which helped recognize the significance of loneliness
3. An expanding awareness through being open to lonely life, including feeling and dialogue
4. A steeping of myself in deeper regions of loneliness; it became the center of my world
5. An intuitive grasping of the patterns of loneliness
6. Further clarification and refinement through study of lonely lives
7. Creation of a form to communicate the results

I will now examine these steps to see which ones can be maintained to establish a general method. To venture into the area of research always means that the question of method will arise. It should be noted that Moustakas (1990) often speaks of heuristic *research* rather than method and describes phases or processes of an entire research investigation instead of steps, as though he is trying to avoid the question of method. However, he also comes around to describe the design and methodology of the heuristic approach, so that however reluctant he may have been to engage with the conventional criteria of methodical research, he finally did speak to his way of conducting research in terms of conventional issues.

It should be noted that in his first review of the steps he utilized to research loneliness that appeared in print, Moustakas (1968) stayed specific to the study. It's as though he was trying to clarify to himself the procedures he lived through but not at all trying to come up with a general method. Our goal in reviewing these steps is to see if a generic method can be determined based on what Moustakas did. If heuristic research is to be a mode of analysis to be practiced by many with different phenomena, then a generic method utilizable by many will have to be articulated. However personal the experiences that form the data base, as subsequent publications show, Moustakas (1968; 1972) did not intend his heuristic research on loneliness to be a one-time event. Consequently, an examination of the original research study may throw light on the possibility of developing a general method.

The first factor that Moustakas (1968) mentions is the personal crisis that created the problem for him. Clearly, this factor cannot be generalized. One cannot claim that all new research must be based upon a personal crisis. Of course, new research may be initiated as a result of a personal crisis, but simple curiosity could also serve the same purpose. Consequently, the first factor cannot be generalized as an essential part of a heuristic method.

The second through fifth steps can be lumped together because they all involve self-reflection and self-exploration even though the themes that emerge differ, and occasional extra-personal references are included (e.g., Step 3 includes "through conversation, dialogue and discussion; Moustakas, 1968, p. 112). But these steps are extremely vague and raise more questions than they answer. Who are the others with whom conversations and dialogues take place? Moustakas also said that he expanded his awareness of loneliness through "being open to lonely life and lonely experiences, through watching, listening and feeling," Are there rules for bringing such feelings into focus? What if awareness of the phenomenon of interest doesn't expand? Does greater depth of feeling always mean greater understanding? Moustakas has admitted that the feeling of loneliness can be frightening. What if the fright blocks further exploration? Moustakas doesn't seem to allow for failures when using the procedures he advocates. Because his personal reflections opened up to greater understanding for him does not guarantee that others will have the same experience. I'm certainly not against reflection and solitary explorations, but more has to be said. His specific comments are simply too vague to allow a method to be articulated. If there is a preferred way of reflecting on and exploring oneself, Moustakas does not give any indication of how it is to be done.

The sixth step more solidly introduces a type of otherness, but it also is too vaguely formulated. How is one to analyze the lonely lives and lonely experiences of others? From his books, one sees that many concrete descriptions are presented, and sometimes comments based upon reflections on the descriptions are offered. But is any published report on loneliness acceptable? Moustakas seems to rely strictly upon qualitative data and analyses. Fair enough. But what is the reason for this preference? Would he study a report on loneliness that used a questionnaire and expressed its results quantitatively, given his aversion to such procedures (Moustakas, 1968, p. 103)? Some minimal description of an acceptable report about the experience of loneliness, or how to obtain such a report, has to be offered.

The seventh and final step is that the results of the study have to be communicated. Moustakas's (1961) book *Loneliness* is one way of expressing the findings. Basically, it contains concrete, specific descriptions of loneliness felt by himself and others, with some reflections on those experiences. One certainly learns many details about the experience of being lonely and can easily be moved by such descriptions. But what one takes away from such data is left to each reader. It is not at all clear that individual readers would come away with what was truly essential about loneliness. Rather, readers would seem to respond to what was written in personally specific ways.

Based on the above analysis, if one tried to summarize the heuristic method employed in the study of loneliness, one would have to say that a researcher has to seek out a certain phenomenon; experience it passionately, deeply, and variedly multiple times; and then try to determine its qualities through self-exploration and self-reflection. It is also helpful to turn to others to get their personal descriptions of the same phenomenon and to dialogue and converse with them. What is highlighted in the above procedures is *what* is to be done, but not *how*. However, methods are equally concerned with how things are done as with *what* is done. While the above procedures, as exemplified by the study on loneliness, communicate emotionally in a significant way, the scientific intellectual achievements, beyond personal relevance, are unclear.

Moustakas (1990) acknowledges that what he started with his book *Loneliness* in 1961 was continued in several other books (Moustakas, 1972 1975), but there is also no discussion of method in these books. Once again there is a strong affirmation of the value of solitude, self-exploration, and meditation in his 1972 book, while the 1975 book consists of letters written by readers who had been impacted by what Moustakas said in his original book. Moustakas again declares in those works that he experienced significant self-awareness and self-growth as a result of experiencing loneliness. It is perhaps time to make explicit a theme that has been lurking behind the scene throughout this presentation. What Moustakas is really after is a way to help individuals use their own experience to help themselves. He is a believer in the value of self-processing and wishes to articulate procedures that will help others achieve that goal. He is also a believer in self-growth and believes that whatever the focus of an internal search might be, self-healing or self-growth is a necessary accompaniment. Moustakas is seeking empathic understanding or personal knowledge and, above all else, believes that the direct path to such an outcome is self-experiential processing. Moustakas is clear that the theme of heuristic inquiry is human experience, but the fact that it is primarily for purposes of healing or helping only comes through after reading all his examples. No wonder Moustakas was impatient with conventional psychological methods. They have neither the same goal nor the same procedures.

One could say that Moustakas's methodical goal is the opposite of the norm. All researchers know that during the course of conducting research, the researchers themselves also grow and learn. That is how experienced researchers happen. But, primarily, what is reported is the results regarding the theme of the research, the reason the research was conducted in the first place. Moustakas seems to reverse these priorities. Primary for him seems to be the researcher's growth and learning, and whatever theme provoked that process is subservient to that goal.

## Further Articulation of the Heuristic Method

All the qualities about heuristic studies that I inferred above are basically confirmed in an article published by Douglass and Moustakas (1985) entitled: "Heuristic Inquiry: The Internal Search to Know." This article contains a systematic effort by the developers or sympathizers of heuristic research to codify its process of inquiry. The authors still refuse to prescribe anything like a "how-to-do" procedure since they seem to value "practice" and concrete experiencing over any clearly articulated instructions. Douglass and Moustakas state that "In its purest form, heuristic inquiry is a passionate and discerning personal involvement in problem solving, an effort to know the essence of some aspect of life through the internal pathways of the self" (1985, p. 39). They also add that heuristic inquiry has "private and imaginative" characteristics that make the method especially challenging and, I would add, difficult to articulate.

I have been trying to make sense of just how the heuristic process is practiced and why it works when it does. The article by Douglass and Moustakas (1985) is helpful in this regard because it highlights certain features of the heuristic inquiry process. First of all, there are the emphases on the self, mentioned numerous times and in varied ways, and the emphases on the experiential process that the researcher undergoes. It is acknowledged that heuristic inquiry is a discovery-oriented method, and while steps are provided, they remain vague. Finally, a contrast with phenomenology is presented, but I will comment on that contrast in the next section.

I am a methodologist and my background is in experimental psychology, so I am conversant with most of the methods of mainstream psychology. However, in my work, I also have found it necessary to break away from the priority of quantitative methods in order to introduce a qualitative method to study the meanings of experience (but more on that later.) Thus, I'm trying to understand what Moustakas did that inspires both admiration and reservations. I think that what Moustakas has started has some built-in assumptions or unclarified aims that are contingent, albeit not essential, so that his overall project is promising but limiting. He doesn't quite bring to a successful closure a method that can be used by many researchers on multiple phenomena. So, let's examine the distinctive features of heuristic inquiry to see if they can be generalized sufficiently to form the basis of a usable method.

## Emphasis on the Self or the Personal

Most methods stress that the method being employed is as neutral as possible. That is, the self or the personhood of the researcher has a minimum effect on the results. This lets readers know that the results reflect the intrinsic features of the phenomenon and are not due to the unintended roles of the researcher. Contrarily, it is rather obvious that heuristic inquiry proudly emphasizes the role of the self or the person in the research process. When reading about heuristic inquiry, one can hardly escape this fact, but I will cite two examples. "Heuristics encourages the researcher to go wide open and to pursue an original path that has its origins within the self and that discovers its direction and meaning within the self" (Douglass & Moustakas, 1985, p. 53). Also, "Learning that proceeds heuristically has a path of its own. It is self-directed, self-motivated, and open to spontaneous shift. It defies the shackles of convention and tradition" (Douglass & Moustakas, p. 44). Thus, the role that the self plays in heuristic research is personal, subjective, and even idiosyncratic, as opposed to the generalized role that usually characterizes traditional research. If the key factors contributing to success are so unique and self-defined, how is one to instruct others how to employ such a method so that it can be successful? It almost seems as though success, if it happens, occurs by chance.

## Heuristics is a Discovery-Oriented Approach

Most research in psychology is performed with verification in mind. That is, the researcher formulates a hypothesis, then collects data under appropriate conditions in order to see if the hypothesis is confirmed or verified. Discovery-oriented research is conducted in order to find out what is going on with certain phenomena. The key factor being sought is how a phenomenon announces itself or how it unfolds. It is an attempt to discover the important dimensions of a phenomenon. It is, if you will, an earlier phase of the research process, although if the findings are strong enough, it is not necessary to follow up with a verification study. I (Giorgi, 1986) argued for this distinction with respect to phenomenological research some time ago. In any case, the discovery motive also distinguishes heuristic inquiry from much of conventional psychological research, but not uniquely so. It is also a feature that is generalizable and can become a descriptive part of a general heuristic method.

## Emphasis on Experiential Processes While Dealing with an Opaque Problem

We have to remember that heuristic inquiry began with Moustakas's experience of loneliness. Because it puzzled him, he decided to probe his own experience of loneliness to see if he could understand it better. The phenomenon was not highlighted in the literature because it did not easily lend itself to the quantitative methods that prevailed at the time. So Moustakas probed, questioned, and examined his own experience of loneliness. He encountered and described some clarities, some ambiguities, some dead-ends, a few breakthroughs, more puzzlements, and some false paths. But according to him, each specific experience was leading him to some understanding of the phenomenon. It is apparent that such descriptions are one of Moustakas's strengths. He's quite good at tracing the vagaries of an experiential process, and in such a way that it opened things up for him. For Moustakas, all the aspects and nuances of his experience contributed to his understanding: his passion, dedication, honesty, intensity, and relentless pursuit of every lead that his experience presented to him. Consequently, the idea occurred to him that others should also try a type of self-analysis and surely would succeed as well. But how is one to generalize something so personal, so intimate? Maybe what Moustakas did requires a special talent that not everyone possesses? Is it really the case that everyone who goes through a difficult experiential process comes out better at the end? How then do we account for failures in therapy? It seems that more than merely suffering an experiential process is needed to account for successful outcomes. Are there no clues for specifying the process in a more adequate way? What clues are there for interpreting certain passages more thoroughly or for bypassing others? More needs to be said if this phase of the inquiry is to be helpful in a general way.

### The Vague Steps of the Method

Douglass and Moustakas (1985) describe the method of heuristic inquiry as consisting of three general steps: "Immersion, Acquisition and Realization" (pp. 45–46). Each step is elaborated slightly, but the terms only indicate a general direction without specifying what is to be sought. The vagueness and brevity of the description of the steps raise many questions, so many that it would extend this article unduly if I had to list them all. Hence, I will only raise a few questions, which could be multiplied many times over. For example, we are told that immersion implies "indwelling, internal frame of reference, and self-search" (1985, p.45). Douglass and Moustakas state that "Self-experience is the single most important guideline in pursuing heuristic research" (p. 46). But even with that sentence there is still an ambiguity. During self-experiencing, do I search myself, or do I search the phenomenon that I am experiencing?

Douglass & Moustakas (1985, p. 53) state that they "have discussed heuristics as a philosophic and conceptual orientation, containing key ideas drawn from existentialism and phenomenology." Intentionality is a key concept of phenomenology, as Moustakas (1988) recognizes, but it is ignored in this discussion. Intentionality means that many acts of consciousness are directed toward objects. Consequently, to say that self-experience is the single most important guideline for heuristics is ambiguous. Do they mean that I must reflect on the series of acts (noeses) that I am living through, or do I reflect on the objects (noemata) that keep presenting themselves to me? Do I search the phenomenon to clarify myself, or do I interrogate the self to clarify the phenomenon? Or do I reflect on each aspect to clarify what is given as it is given? If all variations are necessary, then that should be specified as well.

In other words, while "indwelling, internal frame of reference," and "self-search" may communicate some common meaning in everyday life, these terms are too vague to direct methodical activities. There is constant emphasis on the self, but the self–world relationship is present only through implication and not explicitly acknowledged. The authors constantly emphasize self and experience without making clear that both terms are relational and not substantive (I reflect on myself; experience is of phenomena of the world.) However, by employing the concept of intentionality, further specification is possible. The developers of heuristics did not pursue the effort of methodical clarification to its proper termination.

Many of the same criticisms can be made of the acquisition phase of the research. There is strong emphasis on the tacit, the spontaneous, and subliminal, preconscious perceptions (Douglass & Moustakas, 1985). There seems to be a distrust of what is clear, transparent, and verifiable. Douglass and Moustakas write that, "Tacit knowing operates behind the scenes, giving birth to the hunches and vague, formless insights that characterize heuristic discovery" and "To know, without awareness of how or why one knows, is the sine qua non of tacit knowing" (p. 49). But part of the criteria for scientific research is that any study conducted by one researcher can be replicated by another researcher in another setting. When so much is tacit, vague, formless, and without awareness, how can another researcher replicate the first researcher's study? What the heuristic researcher is confident about is very general and vague: "… the tacit dimension is the forerunner of inference and intuition, guiding the person to untapped aspects of awareness in nonlinear ways that elude analysis or explanation" (Douglass & Moustakas, 1985, p. 49). This implies that even after some degree of success, the original researcher cannot describe or explain why he did what he did. Replication then becomes impossible.

The third and final generic step is what the authors call the "Realization" (Douglass & Moustakas, 1985, p. 52). The realization represents the synthesis of all the findings, and the authors rightly emphasize its holistic character. They stress that the realization is not a summary but the generation of a new reality, a new significance established by the heuristic process But how that step is achieved is not spoken to.

After going through these analyses, what heuristics inquiry is trying to do becomes clearer. It seems to me that there are two difficulties with the way in which Moustakas (1990) and Douglass and Moustakas (1985) try to present the idea of heuristics inquiry as a scientific research method. What is presented is not so much the logic of a scientific method as its *psychology*, and the primary goal of heuristics inquiry is not so much theoretical knowledge as *therapeutic* knowledge—the desire to help. Moustakas is excellent at describing the process of living through the unfolding of an opaque, personal experiential problem until certain clearer manifestations emerge. Moreover, the unfolding process is highlighted according to its capacity to be helpful to oneself or another. Over and over again termination happens when some good has been achieved. The message on the back cover of Moustakas's (1988) book states this purpose explicitly, "The book is a valuable resource in enabling persons to move from despair to hope and from self-denial and defeat to self-affirmation."

The role of the researcher as experiencer of the phenomenon is what makes heuristic inquiry different. Its goal is to resolve some personal problem so that the person feels better. Consequently, maybe it is wrong to judge this procedure by the criteria of scientific methods as I have been doing. Perhaps it has to be judged by therapeutic criteria. But then, Moustakas (1990) himself articulated his method in terms of conventional criteria. Also, it still leaves open-ended the question of whether the interrogation of oneself is done properly even if the goal is therapeutic.

## Phenomenology as Distinct from Heuristic Inquiry

Insofar as I can ascertain, there is no mention of phenomenology by Moustakas until the publication of the article by Douglass and Moustakas (1985). In that article, the authors contrast phenomenology with heuristic inquiry and summarize the phenomenological approach as one that emphasizes subjectivity and is interested in the ordinary phenomena of everyday life (pp. 42–43). They also state that phenomenology focuses on the structure of experiences—I would say that, more accurately, it focuses on concrete experiences in order to come up with structures. The authors also state that phenomenology is interested in the meaning of events and that its approach is unbiased because it brings no presuppositions to its analysis.

All of the above is generally true. But another characteristic assigned to phenomenology by the authors needs correction. They correctly note that the raw data of phenomenological psychological research consists of subjective data—i.e., reports or descriptions from the first-person perspective of various phenomena that have been experienced by ordinary persons. Douglass & Moustakas (1985, p. 43) then state that such data are transformed into "objective accounts of reality." Rather, the analyses result in "structures of experiences" that claim intersubjective validity and depict how certain affairs presented themselves to the experiencers. But because of the reduction, no claim is made that the affairs actually existed the way that they were experienced. Douglass and Moustakas also state that the phenomenological analysis is completed when the essence is revealed "through textural and structural descriptions." It is indeed true that finding the essence of a phenomenon is one of the outcomes sought. But it is the structure that is the essence, and the structure is not obtained by textural and structural descriptions (more on this later).

What is curious here is that no reference is given by the authors to indicate from which source they obtained the details about the phenomenological method as applied to psychology, against which they contrasted heuristics. It looks very similar to the method that I (Giorgi, 1975) outlined, but I cannot be certain.[3] In any case, the authors went on to contrast what they thought were key differences between a phenomenological approach to research in psychology and heuristic inquiry. Moustakas (1994) later repeated differences that were very similar to what was said in 1985, so I will comment on both here. If the 1994 exposition adds something different, I will indicate it.

Douglass and Moustakas (1985) describe four differences between the phenomenological method as applied to psychology and their own use of phenomenology (or heuristics?). The first difference is stated as follows: "Whereas phenomenology encourages a kind of detachment from the phenomenon being investigated, heuristics emphasizes connectedness and relationship" (p. 43). In 1994, Moustakas added that phenomenology limited itself to a description of a situation, whereas in heuristics the participant was allowed to wander far and wide. Heuristics rarely bases its research on one situation.

It is not really clear what the authors mean by phenomenological detachment. As a phenomenological psychological researcher, I can tell you that I am frequently quite engaged with the phenomenon. That is, I am intensely engaged with the phenomenon I am researching but not with the personal characteristics of the experiencer, except to the extent that such characteristics might contribute to the meaning of the phenomenon. If I may bring in the intentional relation again, which is not discussed at all by the authors in their application of phenomenology (although Moustakas talks about intentionality theoretically in his later 1988 book), I am very interested in and quite engaged with the act–object relationship of the experiencer. I am not interested in the particular acts of personal consciousness that I might use to accomplish my analytic tasks. The methodical demand on the analysis I perform is such that any other qualified phenomenological psychological researcher should be able to see what I intuited and confirm it, or else, using her own analysis, offer her data as a critique of what I did. In other words, we are seeking intersubjective or interpersonal findings, not felt dimensions of our own personal processes that somehow stand out for us.

Consequently, I would say that the phenomenological researcher who is seeking the essence of a phenomenon experienced by another has precisely the right kind of engagement. We are doing science, and thus seek to meet its general criteria. At the end of the last section, we saw that heuristics was really a psychological process seeking to help oneself or another. Therefore, the two tasks are not at all identical; they have different purposes and so should use phenomenology in different ways. Neither Douglass nor Moustakas ever refer to the fact that the purposes of the two methods differ and the difference in goals accounts for the differences in procedures.

Moustakas correctly asserts that in the Giorgi method the participant is asked to describe a single situation in which the phenomenon was experienced. A situation is the most proximate way in which others and the world are encountered by persons. It sets definite limits to the description, and limits are desired because we want to be able to trace meaningful connections and influences. Setting reasonable limits helps make the phenomenon stand out, which is our focus. In any case, actual experiences take place in situations. But heuristics is interested in the person, so anything that reveals something about the person is acceptable to them—although if stricter scientific criteria were respected, certain controls would also be employed there. Finally, phenomenological research is also rarely based on the description of a single situation. Almost always, several subjects describing several situations are used. One has to distinguish between an actual research project and an illustrative example.

The second difference according to Douglass and Moustakas (1985) is described as follows: "Whereas phenomenology permits the researcher to conclude with definitive descriptions of the structures of experience, heuristics leads to depictions of essential meanings and portrayal of the intrigue and personal significance that imbue the search to know" (p. 43). Later, Moustakas (1994) added that "heuristics...in addition to narrative descriptions, seeks to obtain self-dialogues, stories, poems, artworks, journals and diaries, and other personal documents that *depict* the experience" (p. 18). However, if, as we said, the structure is the essence of the experience and heuristics wants to depict essential meanings, I don't see how they differ, except possibly in terms of the means used to arrive at what is essential. For heuristics, essences simply seem to appear, whereas for phenomenology they have to be constituted with the help of imaginative variation.

The idea that "the portrayal of the intrigue and personal significance that imbue the search to know" has to be included with research reports, to me, is simply a bias. Or perhaps the idea is important when the goal is to help oneself. But in general, a personal factor is imposed here, where it is not necessary. Is not scientific curiosity sufficient to motivate a research project? Certainly a multitude of scientists have been so motivated. In addition, the solution of a complex theoretical problem—e.g., solving the question of what it means to assume a psychological perspective—can be personally rewarding without having personal significance. A scientist, or even a therapist, can be highly motivated to solve a problem for its own sake even if it holds no personal significance for her. To add the idea of personal significance to the essential characteristics of a good researcher is simply arbitrary. It reflects a personal bias.

The fact that heuristics seeks any form of expression that is produced by the individual is not necessarily an advantage. It introduces complexity because some of those expressions need to be interpreted (e.g. poems, artwork, stories), and Moustakas (1994) argues against interpretation:

> The life experience of the heuristic researcher and the research participants is not a text to be read or interpreted, but a comprehensive story that is portrayed in vivid, alive, accurate and meaningful language and that is further elucidated through poems, songs, artwork, and other personal documents and creations. The depiction is complete in itself. Interpretation not only adds nothing to heuristic knowledge but removes the aliveness and vitality from the nature, roots, meanings, and essences of experience. (p. 19)

It is certainly peculiar to say that artistic forms of expression never require interpretation. Either the artistic forms are extremely simple and banal, or they have depth, which is what heuristics claims to be seeking. But to claim significant depth in an artform that is transparent is highly unlikely.

The authors (Douglass & Moustakas, 1985) describe the third difference as follows: "Whereas phenomenological research generally concludes with the presentation of the distilled structures of experience, heuristics may involve reintegration of derived knowledge that itself is an act of creative discovery, a synthesis that includes intuition and tacit understanding" (p. 43). Later, Moustakas (1994) added that "heuristic research aims toward composite depictions that remain close to the individual stories" (pp. 18–19). However, the structures that phenomenologists discover are the result of the analysis, not the result of the whole research project, because one then dialogues the structure of the research with literature and with the findings of other researchers. Besides, the description of the structure is itself a creative task. It is not easily done and may take extraordinary powers of intuition to capture it well.

Douglass and Moustakas say that their results include "intuiting." Unless they mean something different, all phenomenological results are based on intuitions. Finally, insofar as during the process of intuiting a structure, one concentrates on the outcome and not on the process, one can easily say that certain modes of tacit understanding are being employed. All the differences posited by the authors under their third point disappear except for their emphasis on composite descriptions that stay close to the individual stories. Phenomenological findings are essential and general, but that does not prevent phenomenological researchers from speaking about particulars because they are all implied in the essential description. If heuristic results stay close to the particular, how do they get to the essence of the person that they also claim to describe?

The fourth difference cited by Douglass and Moustakas (1985) states:

> Whereas phenomenology loses the persons in the process of descriptive analysis, in heuristics the research participants remain visible in the examination of the data and continue to be portrayed as whole persons. Phenomenology ends in the essence of experience; heuristics retains the essence of the person in experience. (p. 43)

The same point is repeated later. Douglass and Moustakas seem to forget that a structure represents a relationship; a conscious act directed toward an object or a human subject engaged with the world. The essential aspects of personhood for an experience to take place are included. What is not included is the individuality of the person having the experience. But that is true of all scientific psychological research. For good reasons, we never know all the individual details of persons who serve as participants in psychological investigations. However, we often do know many personal details about persons who serve as examples in clinical or therapeutic analyses because such details are relevant for comprehending the difficulties the persons are experiencing. Thus, in articulating this difference, the authors do not take into account the purpose of the research. They seek more personal details because they have therapeutic interests in mind; scientific phenomenological researchers seek essential understanding of the way phenomena are experienced by persons.

To say that "Phenomenology ends with the essence of the experience" (Douglass & Moustakas, 1985, p. 43) is to say that the essential personal characteristics necessary in order for an experience to take place are included. Moreover, is the essence of the person retained in heuristics, or is it rather that certain emotional, personal details are included while the person is confronting some difficult problem? For example, Moustakas (1968, p. ix) writes, "I have gone out beyond what I have known, in doubt, in uncertainty, in shock; I have faced the extremes of feelings in anger, in joy, in suffering, in passion. I have wept with others in long hours of agony, and the tears have dissipated into laughter and I have laughed with others into tears of ecstasy." That is part of a long description by Moustakas that continues in the same vein as he struggled with the issue of how to retain his individuality while contemplating the theme of "the individual in mass society." But is that the essence of Moustakas? Or is he rather describing the emotional ups and downs he encountered while trying to find a solution to the issue of retaining an individual perspective while surrounded by a society that tries to stifle individuality Once again, the relational aspect of experiencing is missing. Moustakas was undergoing such experiences while he was confronting a phenomenal world that was showing different faces of itself, and he reacted accordingly. Maybe he drew from his essential self, but his essence was not articulated in a clear way.

With respect to the contrast between phenomenology and heuristics as articulated by Douglass and Moustakas (1985), my conclusions are as follows:

1. Phenomenologists are just as connected to the data as are heuristic researchers, except that scientific phenomenologists are connected to the relationship between the experiencer and the situation and not just to the self or other that heuristics researchers emphasize—and especially not to the experiences that the researcher herself undergoes as she conducts the research.

2. When phenomenologists communicate experiential structures, they are communicating essential meanings that were obtained by means of a methodical process. Heuristic researchers claim to communicate essential meanings, but they imply that they are simply there to be described. They never demonstrate the role of imaginative variation. But for phenomenology, essences have to be constituted by a specific method. Furthermore, whether the research was initiated by an event with personal significance or by a theoretical motive is irrelevant for phenomenology, although the former motive is critical for heuristics.

3. After discussion of the third point, the alleged differences between phenomenology and heuristics disappear except for the emphasis on the particulars of the person that heuristics seeks. Phenomenology in its analyses uses intuition and tacit understanding, and it is as creative as heuristics claims to be.

4. The essential structures provided by phenomenology as part of its results include the active participation of human personhood, so the person is not missing in phenomenological results. Heuristics claims to contain the essence of the person in its analyses, but that essence is never articulated. Rather, one gets the emotional particulars of the participant dialoguing with the world, which are too particular to be parts of an essential description.

## Moustakas's Phenomenological Method

As previously mentioned, the first time I became aware of Moustakas's interest in phenomenology was when he and Douglass (1985) contrasted a specific application of phenomenology to psychological research (which was mine) with his own heuristic method. The next time the term appeared, it was used to articulate a method for researching problems in which Moustakas (1988, 1994) was interested. I'm not sure what precipitated the change, and Moustakas does not speak directly to the change in attitude toward phenomenology. He is also silent with respect to the relationship between his earlier heuristic method and the phenomenological method he developed later. However, the types of phenomena that had been, or were about to be, researched by both methods remain highly similar, if not identical. For example, in presenting the phenomena that heuristic researchers have studied, Moustakas (1990, pp. 59–70) lists, "Really feeling connected to nature; transforming self-doubt into self-confidence; the depiction of self-doubt; the mother–daughter relationship; the experience of mystery in everyday life; the experience of self-reclamation;" and so on. In his first phenomenological book, Moustakas (1988) states explicitly that he developed

> a model of psychotherapy that offers a methodology for dealing with concrete issues and problems of everyday experience, a model that guides the resolution of disturbing relationships, distorted communications, experiences of depression, grief, loneliness, hostility, and human misery and suffering. The model is problem-centered and follows a system that is flexible yet sufficiently structured to guide a therapy process in contending with conflicts, tensions, and issues that have blocked awareness and understanding, interfered with action, and prevented the use of self-resources. (pp. vii–viii)

The phenomena appear to be more or less the same, but with his phenomenological method Moustakas is more explicit about its use as a method for helping the researcher resolve an experiential problem or for helping persons who are in distress.

Before examining the method directly, some comments regarding Moustakas's style of scholarship and learning are necessary. Moustakas (1988) tells us that he is pretty much a self–directed learner. Here is how he describes his mode of learning or study:

> As far back as I can remember I have sought to know the truth of things through my own intuition and perception, learning from my own direct experience and from awareness and reflections that would bring meanings to light. My natural bent was to avoid people who tried to instruct me from their facts and knowings, and to approach things for the first time alone, preferably when no one was around. I have always wanted to encounter life freshly, to allow myself to be immersed in

situations in such a way that I could see, really see and know from my own vision and from the images and voices within. Somehow, being alone freed me to an open and unfettered view of whatever was before me. I could concern myself only with what I was encountering, a private relationship, free to be, to learn and to know. The most significant understandings I have come to, have not grown themselves from books or from others, but initially at least from my own direct perceptions and intuitions. This has been true of my teaching, my therapy, intimate relationships in my life, my involvement as a parent, as a person in the everyday world. The most crucial learnings have come from a lonely separation from the natural world, from an immersion and self-dialogue, from a transcendental place of knowing and being. (p. 18)

In learning about phenomenology Moustakas read Husserl many times as well as many philosophical commentators on Husserl, and he dialogued with colleagues, students, and friends. But in the last analysis, he had to depend upon his own intuitions. Moustakas (1988) stated:

In this process (of learning Husserlian phenomenology), certain concepts and values stood out for me. I sought to place myself purely in Husserl's world of transcendental phenomenology, while recognizing that my own knowledge and experience, in a free, open and imaginative sense, ultimately would determine the core ideas and values that would linger and endure. (p. 1)

What Moustakas described about himself is in many ways praiseworthy. It also fits in with the American spirit, the idea of a man who does not follow the beaten path and who forges a new path to important discoveries based upon his own resources. It's the idea of the determined, self-reliant man who, against all opposition, achieves a goal that is good for many.

But one has to wonder whether these characteristics are universally good or best suited for certain circumstances. There is a difference, after all, between directly experiencing the phenomena of the world and reading and studying philosophical texts. Moustakas was a psychologist, so he was prepared to flow with experiential processes that determined the contents of the heuristic method and, when necessary, to challenge them or interrogate them until the meanings they were conveying became clear to him. But the only way he could get the sense of phenomenological philosophy was through the texts of Husserl and his commentators. Of course, he could have sat in on courses on phenomenological philosophy given by philosophers, but there is no indication that he did so. Being a non-philosopher, it is possible that he did not grasp everything that Husserl wrote in the way that Husserl intended for it to be understood. After all, when learning a system of thought, it is incumbent upon the learner to articulate that system the way that the originator would want it to be presented.

There is evidence that there are certain flaws in how Moustakas presents phenomenology, which makes the underpinnings of his method suspect. There are certain limitations in his presentation of phenomenology that need to be addressed. In addition, when he carries over certain phenomenological principles into concrete methodical steps, it's not always obvious that phenomenological criteria are maintained. To be clear, whenever Moustakas quotes Husserl or other commentators, he does so correctly. It is when he begins paraphrasing or explicating some of the notions that he sometimes miscommunicates. At the very least, I think that it is necessary to point out three critical misunderstandings in his presentation of transcendental phenomenology.

## The Idea of Transcendental Phenomenology

Moustakas claims that he is practicing Husserlian transcendental phenomenology and calls it a science, although at times he correctly expresses it as being a model for developing human science methods. But more often than not he sees it as a science. Thus, Moustakas (1988) writes, "Husserl's phenomenology is a Transcendental Phenomenology, in essence a new theory of science" (p. 23), and "To summarize transcendental phenomenology is a scientific study of the appearance of things, of phenomena just as we see them and as they appear to us in consciousness" (Moustakas, 1994, p. 49). Actually, transcendental phenomenology is strictly a philosophy. It's true that Husserl wants philosophy to be a strict science, but what he means is that philosophy should be as rigorous in its work as science is in its work. But that doesn't mean that philosophy becomes a science. It means that it should practice its craft as rigorously as science practices its own modes of gaining knowledge. Husserl (1997) even uses the expression "transcendental science" occasionally, but he clearly means "philosophy as science" (p. 493) since he refers to Fichte as one who understood its "pure meaning," whereas Moustakas uses the term in the sense of a positive science of psychology. However, the two projects, philosophy and science, are quite different.

More important, however, Moustakas seems not to understand that the transcendental ego in Husserl is not a human ego. He writes that "Husserl's transcendental science offers a carefully developed conceptual model that brings the person back as the necessary source for explicating experience and deriving knowledge" (1988, pp. 26–27). He also wrote:

> The challenge of transcendental phenomenology was to develop a method for understanding the objects that appear before us. Such a science requires a return to the self and employment of a self-reflective process that enables the searcher increasingly to know herself or himself within the experience being investigated. (1994, p. 47)

However, Husserl (1960) writes:

> By phenomenological epoché I reduce my natural human Ego and my psychic life—the realm of *my psychological self-experience*—to my transcendental-phenomenological Ego, the realm of *transcendental-phenomenological self-experience*. The Objective world, the world that exists for me, that always has and always will exist for me, the only world that ever can exist for me—this world, with all its Objects, I said, derives whole sense and its existential status, which it has for me, from me myself, *from me as the transcendental Ego*, the Ego who comes to the fore only with transcendental-phenomenological epoché. (p. 26, italics in original)

To make his point clear, Husserl (1960, p. 25) adds, "This Ego, with his Ego-life, who necessarily remains for me, by virtue of such epoché, is not a piece of the world; and if he says, 'I exist, ego cogito,' that no longer signifies, 'I, this man, exist'" (p. 25). What remains is a pure ego, an ego that represents any possible consciousness. Thus, it transcends any possible human mode of being conscious. In fact, so critical is this notion that Bruzina (2004) refers to Fink's characterization of the transcendental phenomenological reduction as "un-humanization." For Husserl, all psychological science takes place within the natural attitude. Consequently, the perspective cannot be transcendental.

In addition, Moustakas nowhere refers to Husserl's (1977) lectures on phenomenological psychology. In that work, Husserl introduces the phenomenological psychological reduction, which is not transcendental and which functions within the natural attitude. Within that reduction, the objects of consciousness are reduced, but the acts can be considered human acts because the transcendental reduction is not employed. Consequently, one can then claim that when analyzing human consciousnesses we are indeed dealing with human persons in the world. Moustakas may have naively operated in this mode since he always presumed a human consciousness, although the status of the object is not always clear. It is hard to figure out whether it is reduced or not.

## Understanding Phenomenological Reduction

While Moustakas (1994, 1988) frequently refers to the phenomenological reduction, he mostly talks about the bracketing of presuppositions or horizonalization without ever making explicit what the reduction actually accomplishes. There are expressions in his books that correctly state that after the reduction, the researcher is dealing with a phenomenon (e.g., Moustakas, 1994) but it is not clear that Moustakas knows how this status is achieved. For example, nowhere in his books does he directly state what the reduction accomplishes: It withholds the positing of the existence of what is given so that the given is considered as something that is merely present to consciousness. Consequently, what may be actually and really given is considered within the reduction to be merely a presence.

Instead of such a clear statement, here are some samples of how Moustakas (1994) speaks about the phenomenological reduction: (a) "In the Transcendental-Phenomenological Reduction, each experience is considered in its singularity, in and for itself" (p. 34); (b) "Ultimately, through the Transcendental-Phenomenological Reduction we derive a textural description of the meanings and essences of the phenomenon...."; (c) "the process (Phenomenological Reduction) involves a prereflective description of things just as they appear and a reduction to what is horizontal and thematic" (p. 91); (d) "'Reduction' in that it leads us back to our own experience of the way things are (Schmitt, 1968, p. 30)" (Moustakas, 1994, p. 91); (e) "In Phenomenological Reduction we return to the self; we experience things that exist in the world from the vantage point of self-awareness, self-reflection and self-knowledge" (p. 95), and finally (f) Moustakas writes

> To summarize, the steps of the Phenomenological Reduction include *Bracketing....; horizonalizing*, every statement is initially treated as having equal value. Later, statements irrelevant to the topic and question as well as those that are repetitious or overlapping are deleted, leaving only the *Horizons* (the textural meanings and invariant constituents of the phenomenon;) Clustering *the Horizons into Themes*, and *Organizing the Horizons and Themes Into a Coherent Textural Description* of the phenomenon. (p. 97, italics in original)

If we review these statements, we see that the basic meaning of the phenomenological reduction is not touched upon. In (a) Moustakas says that the experience considered within the reduction is "singular." Perhaps; but that is not what the reduction is all about. In (b) he says that the reduction provides a "textural description of the meanings and essences of the phenomenon." The term textural is brought in, and while it may apply to the very initial description of the given, it cannot apply to the essence. The essence is a second-order description essentially different from the initial perception. Also, the impression is given that an essence can be simply described, but it has to be constituted by a methodical procedure. In (c) Moustakas emphasizes that in the reduction one arrives at what is "horizontal and thematic." While a horizon of the given may be explored in the reduction, that is not its primary purpose. Primarily, one withholds the existential affirmation of the given if it is real and concentrates on the given and describes it fully. Then, perhaps, some horizons may be pursued. In any case, the given is not reduced to a theme. In addition, in using the word "things," it is clear that the positing of the existence of the given is not withheld. In (d) Moustakas quotes Schmitt (1968), who apparently states that in the reduction we are led back to "our own experience of the way things are." But who is "our"? Moustakas always speaks from the transcendental perspective and, as we noted, the conscious experiencer there is not a human being. It is any possible consciousness. Again, the term "things" is used, which indicates that the reduction to phenomena has not taken place. In (e) Moustakas states that the reduction leads us back to the self, without clarifying the sense of self being employed. He reiterates that what are given are "things in the world" rather than phenomena. And it is clear that the self that becomes aware, reflects, and has knowledge is a human self, which is incorrect for a transcendental perspective. Finally, in (f) Moustakas gives a summary of the steps of his procedure. Certainly, bracketing is correct, but he gives horizonalizing a rather peculiar meaning; he uses it to say that all that is present to consciousness is initially of equal value. While that is true, it is due to the reduction, not horizonalizing. When Husserl uses horizon, he means that whatever is given in experience is given against a background or within a context. What is given is not just a raw figure, but a figure against a background.

Then Moustakas describes some procedural steps that are not necessarily correct from a phenomenological perspective. He is correct to start by saying that initially every statement has equal value. He is also correct to say that irrelevant statements can be eliminated. But he fails to mention how the irrelevancy of a statement can be established. Not all seemingly irrelevant statements are genuinely irrelevant. Here is where horizonal explorations become important: It often can be shown that seemingly irrelevant statements do have a meaningful connection to whatever else is being said. Also, it's not true that repetitions and overlapping statements should be eliminated. From a psychological perspective, redundancies can be meaningful and should be probed.

Moustakas concludes by saying that one ends up with "horizons which are textural meanings and invariant constituents of the phenomenon." It is not clear why the so-called "textural meanings" and invariant constituents are called "horizons." The primary findings should deal with the given as well as the horizons. Also, if we are presenting findings, we are beyond "textural descriptions," which represent the original data. Plus, invariant constituents are constituted, not given, and how they are constituted is never spoken to. Finally, phenomenological analyses are not thematic analyses. They are holistic analyses that can highlight certain constituents of a structure; however, the constituents are interdependent moments of the structure. They are not themes because they cannot stand isolatedly.

Nowhere in the above elaborations of the reduction does Moustakas mention its genuine meaning: the withholding of the existential affirmation of the given.

### Keen's Influence
In many places Moustakas (e.g., 1988, 1994) speaks about textural and structural descriptions. The problem is that the term texture never

appears in Husserl. Moustakas actually got the term from Ernest Keen (1975), and he utilized it throughout all his writings.[4]

Keen was a psychologist who was also interested in applying phenomenological philosophy to psychological research. While he started off following Husserlian expositions of phenomenology, he did not limit himself to the Husserlian perspective in his writing. For some reason, Keen wanted to call the initial description of a phenomenon a textural description, and he distinguished it from a structure. According to Keen (1975), "*Texture*....is the feel and shape of experience as it is experienced, naively and immediately. *Structure* is that order imbedded within everyday experience which can be grasped only through reflection...." (p. 46, italics in original). Keen then goes on to use "texture" more and more rather than the term "description, which Husserl used, so much so that it became a technical term for him. Keen (1975, p. 58) goes on to say that "....a phenomenological description itself must proceed in a dialectical fashion between structure and texture, each fulfilling the other" (p. 58). Keen also speaks of them as interlocking and mutually implicatory, and then refers to a Heideggerian interpretation of their relationship. He ends up saying, "The concepts of structure and texture are attempts to point to poles of the dialectic, or better, way stations in the phenomenological excursion of the hermeneutic circle" (pp. 59–60). The difficulty with this exposition is that the use of the term "dialectic" specifies a relationship between texture and structure, whereas phenomenology is meant to be presuppositionless.

Speake's (1979) dictionary of philosophy indicates that the term dialectic has a long history in philosophy, but the most contemporary is Hegel's definition. For Speakes, "dialectic is Hegel's name for the logical pattern that thought must follow. Broadly, Hegel argued that thought proceeded by contradiction and the reconciliation of contradiction, the overall pattern being one of thesis, antithesis, and synthesis" (p. 94). Husserl's relationship between an original description and the ultimate structure does not follow that pattern. The original description is the basis of the structure, but once the structure is obtained, there is no need to go back to the original description. Following Keen, Moustakas (1994) speaks about "a synthesis of textural and structural meanings and essences" (p. 104), but such a synthesis is not how essences are determined. Such descriptions are inconsistent with Husserlian phenomenology, as is the idea of a hermeneutic circle.

**Review of Moustakas's Phenomenological Method**
We have seen that Moustakas's exposition of phenomenological philosophy was spotty. Many of its tenets were correctly expressed, but there were also some misunderstandings. In his latest phenomenological work, Moustakas detailed what he called his phenomenological method. We shall review his methodical steps from two perspectives: to determine to what extent they are consistent with phenomenological criteria and to see how they compare with his earlier heuristic method.

Moustakas (1994, pp. 103–104) lists the seven steps of his phenomenological method. We will follow that sequence and comment on any elaborations provided in subsequent pages. Moustakas's first step is: "Discovering a topic and question rooted in autobiographical meanings and values, as well as involving social meanings and significance." Moustakas reinforces this notion when he states that "Personal history brings the core of the problem into focus" (p. 104). From a strict phenomenological perspective, the topic or problem need not be rooted in autobiographical meanings. Critical theoretical or methodical issues can also be motives for conducting research, even for therapeutic phenomena. For example, I may want to know whether immediate feedback or delayed feedback is more helpful to a person who is in a state of emotional turmoil. I might try to research an answer to that problem without being passionately interested in the outcome. That is, I have no personal investment in either option. I'm simply interested in knowing what would be more helpful to the client.

Moustakas clearly carries over this idea from his heuristic method. Insofar as his heuristic method was not directly under the guidance of phenomenological criteria, it was acceptable to posit that criterion for heuristics, but even there I would say that it is allowable but not necessary. Research could still be done on oneself without a passionate interest in the problem. We have to remember that Moustakas began his search for a method while undergoing a deeply emotional experience concerning a serious personal problem. Consequently, passionate personal involvement with the issue was how he experienced the beginning of his method. But it is not hard to get some distance from his personal starting point and see that it is possible to research an aspect of personal experience without strong emotional investment. I'm not saying that the condition of personal emotional investment blocks the possibility of research, although it may introduce some complicating factors. I'm only saying that it is not a necessary requirement even for heuristic research, and certainly not for phenomenological research.

The second step that Moustakas (1994) lists is "Conducting a comprehensive review of the professional and research literature" (p. 103). This step raises no questions. It is necessary for both phenomenological and heuristics research.

The third step is "Constructing a set of criteria to locate appropriate researchers" (Moustakas, 1994, p. 103). The key factor here is that the research participant must have experienced the phenomenon in which the researcher is interested. Sometimes idiosyncratic experiences demand special requirements; then one has to be sure that the participant meets the requirements. In addition, heuristics requires that the researcher has experienced, or will participate in the experience of, the same phenomenon. Heuristics' strong bias in favor of experiencing places that demand on researchers, but it is not at all necessary for phenomenology.

In the fourth step Moustakas, (1994) emphasizes all the demands that ethics imposes on researchers. Phenomenology and heuristics are both in agreement with that principle. The phenomenological perspective insists that if there is a conflict between ethics and science, ethics wins. Heuristics surely agrees.

Steps 5 and 6 will be discussed together: They are (5) developing topics for an interview and (6) conducting a lengthy interview (Moustakas, 1994). It is true that the ability to conduct a good interview is an art and the better the interview, the better the description of the phenomenon. And the better the description, the better the potentiality for understanding what was lived through. My own bias is simply to interview the participant with only mental preparation. But if listing potential questions will help the researcher get better data, then the researcher should use them. The ultimate goal of an interview is to get good data, and anything within reason that helps that goal is allowable.

The seventh and last step, Moustakas (1994) writes, is: "Organizing and analyzing the data to facilitate development of individual textural and structural descriptions, a composite textural description, a composite structural description, and a synthesis of textural and structural meanings and essences" (p. 104). Moustakas is describing multiple types of results here, but not all of them are necessary all the time. If one wants general results, then structural descriptions, or essences, will suffice. If one seeks particular results, then individual structures will do. However, one problem is that

Moustakas carries over here the distinction that Keen made between textural and structural. Textural refers to the original, natural attitude description. But once the phenomenological analysis starts, that description is left behind; it is not integrated into the structural or essential finding because textural and structural description represent two orders of description. The so-called textural description is natural attitude, and the structural description is essential and phenomenological. Essential findings require the application of the method of free imaginative variation, which produces eidetic findings, whereas the so-called textural descriptions are empirical. Moustakas is not at all clear on how and when imaginative variation is to be employed in his approach. He rarely details the actual application of his method (i.e., the actual processes employed) and mostly provides us with a schema of his steps or with examples of results.

Consequently, Moustakas's articulation and practice of a phenomenological method has some serious flaws. He carried over into his phenomenological method some features of his heuristic method, which do not belong in the phenomenological approach. Moreover, he failed to articulate correctly certain steps of the phenomenological method. His development of the heuristic method was not intended to be guided by phenomenology and is extremely personal in nature. Yet Moustakas carried into his phenomenological method two features of his heuristic method that do not properly belong within phenomenology: the fact that the topic being researched has to have personal and biographical relevance to the researcher, and the notion that the researcher must have personally experienced the phenomenon being researched. It is possible that a phenomenon may have great personal significance for a researcher, but it is not a necessary requirement for doing phenomenological research. In addition, the two key features of the phenomenological approach, the use of the reduction and the establishment of essences, are not correctly articulated. The latter failure is due in part because Moustakas was unduly influenced by Keen's approach to phenomenology, which was not strictly Husserlian.

A final limitation of Moustakas's approach is the nature of his descriptive data. He always operated without proper use of the reduction, although he sometimes thought he was utilizing the reduction. In order to apply the reduction correctly, one would have to make full use of the functional characteristics of consciousness. As stated previously, Moustakas talked about these features theoretically, but he seemed unable to apply them correctly.

We shall now turn to certain important characteristics of consciousness upheld by phenomenology.

## Intentional Consciousness

When Brentano (1973) introduced intentionality as a significant aspect of consciousness, he changed the emphasis on how the mind was to be understood. Brentano knew that the scholastic philosophers had used the term to help explain how the mind worked, and he elaborated their conception. Moustakas acknowledged the term theoretically, but he did not exploit its power when he analyzed his own experiences. A correct understanding of intentionality would be extremely helpful in the analysis of experiences—one's own or that of others—because it is a primary determiner of the functioning of consciousness.

Intentionality refers to the fact that many acts of consciousness are directed toward objects, whether external or internal to consciousness. Brentano's (1973) phrasing was, "Every mental phenomenon is characterized by what the Scholastics of the Middle Ages called the intentional (or mental) inexistence of an object...." (p. 88). Brentano was trying to distinguish the object of psychological research from the objects of the physical sciences, and he thought that he had achieved his goal with the notion of consciousness as intentional. The term brought with it certain difficulties, which Brentano tried to clarify and are today mostly of historical interest. More important for us today is that Husserl took over the term and made it a key part of his phenomenology.

Husserl introduced phenomenological distinctions with respect to intentionality that are not in Brentano. We shall follow Mohanty's (1972) analysis of the major differences between Husserl's use of the term and Brentano's. First of all, Husserl was not interested in using intentionality as a term to distinguish psychological objects from physical objects. Second Husserl uses intentionality as the distinguishing feature of conscious acts since not all modes of conscious experiences are intentional. Husserl then clarifies what Brentano referred to as an "immanent object." As Mohanty (1972) expresses it, "It is surely misleading to say that the object enters into or appears within consciousness, or that consciousness contains its object within itself. It is also misleading to say...that consciousness enters into a sort of relationship with its object. (p. 52)

Intentionality is not a real process or a real relation. When a conscious act is intentional, the object toward which the intention is directed is only meant. The object may not exist. "It is only the Erlebnis (the experience or conscious act) that is present, and the Erlebnis has a certain descriptive character, the character of an intention" (Mohanty, 1972, p. 52).

Consciousness also presents itself with other characteristics. A key feature of consciousness is that every lived act of consciousness is intrinsically and concomitantly aware of itself. This is known as the reflexive nature of consciousness. Because of this reflexivity consciousness is able to reflect upon its prereflective activity. Reflexivity is not reflection; it is a non-reflective concomitant awareness. Reflection refers to the capability that consciousness has to look upon its prereflective activity, make it a reflected-upon object, and examine its characteristics. One type of reflection that can take place is called inner perception. Ordinary perception is the perception of an object that is in the world and available to others. Inner perception shifts the focus from the outer object to its mode of givenness for an individual consciousness. The focus of inner perception is strictly on whatever is given within consciousness, regardless of what the outer perception was like, since the object of inner perception differs from the object of outer perception. These processes can take place under two attitudes: the natural attitude and the phenomenological attitude. Brentano worked within the natural attitude, and Husserl introduced the phenomenological attitude as a more rigorous procedure.

Because the analysis within the phenomenological attitude differs from the one conducted within the natural attitude, Husserl, at the transcendental, philosophical level, gave different names to the key parts that are dealt with in the phenomenological attitude: The conscious act is called the noesis, and the object side of intentionality is known as the noema. So noetic–noematic analyses are performed within the phenomenological attitude. The noesis and the noema are correlated terms, which means every change in one term implies a change in the content of the other. However, at the psychological level, which is phenomenological but pre-transcendental, we still speak of act–object relations. We have to correlate the object of the intentional act with the act that initiated the intentional relationship. The analysis continues in this correlational way until the sense of the act is clarified.

Consequently, if a phenomenological method is to be employed, there would have to be act–object analyses of reduced data. The givens on the object side would be reduced to presences, but since the analysis is psychological, the acts would be interpreted as acts of a human consciousness. The original data (if not phenomenologically described) would have to be articulated by a perspective or purpose that is immanent to the consciousness of the researcher. This implies a certain transformation of the original realistic data. For example, if one were to search one of Moustakas's descriptions for something that will help the describer in his distress, the phenomenal way in which that segment of the data would appear to the researcher has to be described as such. It may appear quite differently from the way the original realistic description appeared. Ultimately, it is how the data become phenomenal in the eyes of the researcher that matters.

A final complication presents itself with respect to the way that Moustakas conceived of both his heuristic method and his phenomenological method. It seems that there is always a dual purpose being sought: a clarification of a phenomenon and an awareness of the transformation of self. Thus, Moustakas really wanted to understand the loneliness that was happening to him. He also says that in heuristic research "I am not only lifting out the essential meanings of an experience, but I am actively awakening and transforming my own self" (Moustakas, 1990, p. 13). With respect to his phenomenological method, Moustakas (1994, p. 59) writes: "In a phenomenological investigation the researcher has a personal interest in whatever she or he seeks to know; the researcher is intimately connected with the phenomenon. The puzzlement is autobiographical, making memory and history essential dimensions of discovery...." Thus, the theme of personal self-healing is as important as the clarification of a phenomenon. This duality often means that the pursuit of one goal may take one away from the pursuit of the other, or result in a synthesis of the two. For example, it may mean that the so-called essence of loneliness is really the aspect of loneliness that is most helpful for the researcher's healing. Such a consequence would be very helpful to the researcher, but it would not provide a genuine essence of loneliness.

It is one thing if self-transformation would happen automatically, but in Moustakas's view one is encouraged to pursue it if it is noticed, and that does mean that the clarification of the phenomenon may be neglected. So, the theoretical question is: How good is dual-purposed research? Are the two goals always harmonious, or might the pursuit of one inhibit the clarification of the other? Is there a design feature that would prevent such a dichotomy from happening? Can a researcher maintain equal interest in the two goals? Unfortunately, Moustakas neither speaks to nor clarifies the duality issue. He operates on the assumption that working on one goal (phenomenon clarification) automatically will be helpful to the second goal (self-help) or vice-versa.

A difficulty in evaluating Moustakas's methodical procedures is that in none of his works (Moustakas, 1961, 1990, 1994) does he present a complete study that followed all of his steps. Mostly, he provides summaries or excerpts that substantiate theoretical points, but one never sees how raw data is transformed into psychological interpretations. The excerpts he provides are too decontextualized to evaluate properly. I suppose that one would have to go to the dissertations he directed in order to see the detailed procedures. However, going to dissertations is too big a project for this article and, in any case, there is still the problem of the dual purpose, even for therapeutic or self-help type of research.

I think that it should be clear that dual-purpose research as practiced by Moustakas is not satisfactory. The intermingling of the two purposes makes the whole process confusing and unsystematic. If one wanted to maintain the dual-purpose structure, then one would have to introduce specific procedures for dealing with the two purposes. A precedent for such an approach is provided by Brown et al. (1989). The researchers in this study wanted to understand moral conflicts and the choices that took place during such conflicts. They obtained long narratives from their participants, and when it came time to analyze their descriptions, they realized that they had a series of questions in mind that would require several readings. Because of their multiple interests, they also realized that they would have to read the narratives at least four times. Brown and colleagues (1989, p. 148) stated, "Each reading serves to identify a different aspect of the narrative deemed relevant in locating self and ascertaining moral voice." Thus, they read the same narrative, first, to simply establish the story; second, to identify the "speaking voice" of the agent; third, to highlight the "care voice;" and, last, to determine the "justice voice." The authors argued (pp. 147–148) that "each voice has its own psychological 'logic,' its own psychic legitimacy and organization that can be followed in narratives of moral conflict and choice." In the same manner, then, the tracking of the phenomenon (loneliness) and the tracking of self-help should take place separately. In that way, each purpose is given its due.

## Conclusion

I wanted to examine the methodological work of Clark Moustakas because I was aware that he used self-reports in his research. When I first encountered the task of attempting to do qualitative research with humans about a half-century ago, I deliberately avoided providing my own descriptions of experiential phenomena and then analyzing them myself. I was aware that mainstream research psychologists could ask a question that would sidetrack the whole effort. The question was: "How do I know that your data is not unconsciously in the service of your theory of the phenomenon?" So I developed a method that was based upon first-person descriptions provided by others who knew nothing about my viewpoint so that I could not be accused of using data sympathetic to my views. I then analyzed the descriptions from others from a first-person perspective to the extent possible. My research criteria were highly influenced by the experimental, psychophysical tradition in which I was trained in the 1950s.

Moustakas, involved more with that part of psychology that seeks to help others rather than gain theoretical knowledge, apparently had no reservations about using first-person descriptions, even his own. However, his effort did not begin with the attempt to invent a method but to solve a personal problem. Only after Moustakas realized that he was gaining some insight into his personal problem that was helpful to him did he take up the issue of method. If his own descriptions of his problems were giving him insights and helping him, perhaps what he was doing could be a way of helping others as well. He then began to see what type of method could be formulated and projected onto the heuristic method most of the specific characteristics that he experienced while clarifying loneliness and helping himself. But, as we saw above, the heuristic method failed to meet some of the conventional criteria accepted by most methodologists. Actually, it was an empirical method that seemed more to follow procedures performed by therapists (descriptions of idiographic experiences, seeking solutions to personal problems, research with a dual purpose, termination when self or other is helped) than by researchers seeking theoretical knowledge.

Then, for some reason that is not entirely clear, Moustakas went to Husserlian phenomenological philosophy to found and support a phenomenological psychological method. Two problems developed with this approach. He brought into the articulation of his phenomenological method some features of his earlier heuristic method that did not meet phenomenological criteria. In addition, his grasp of Husserlian philosophy was faulty, and his articulation of the steps required to practice a phenomenological approach were not entirely correct. His approach was again basically empirical, even though phenomenological terms were applied to some of his steps.

To answer the basic question: Yes, it is possible to investigate oneself psychologically. But to do it phenomenologically the following steps would have to be taken. First, one would have to describe carefully precisely what one was experiencing while living through a situation. This description is the empirical description. Second, one would have to adopt the attitude of the phenomenological psychological reduction. This means that the objects of the experience now become phenomena, but the acts are considered to be acts of a human consciousness because we have not left the natural attitude. Third, in addition, all knowledge based on real world or natural attitude accomplishments are bracketed. All knowledge achievements have to be based on whatever is given to consciousness. Fourth, one then concentrates on the object as it is intended by the act and describes its presence. This includes the manner in which the given is present as well as its modality—as remembered, perceived, imagined, and so on. Fifth, one uses the method of imaginative variation in order to come up with the essence of the experience. The description of the essence concludes the investigatory process.

## NOTES

1 Clark Moustakas and I met late in our respective careers. We worked together a bit on a project sponsored by Humanistic Psychology. At the time we worked together, I had no idea that he had an interest in phenomenology, and if he knew about my interest, he never mentioned it to me. I consider him to be a colleague and a friend. Consequently, it is with some hesitation that I bring up some criticisms of his idea of heuristic research and his approach to phenomenology. It is not easy for non-philosophers to grasp phenomenological philosophy—especially Husserl's—correctly.

We psychologists sometimes bring naïve (i.e., non-philosophical) interpretations to phenomenology because of the lack of a proper background. But it is also the case that we must apply phenomenological concepts to psychological problems and procedures because of their intrinsic value, and there is no established guide for such a task. Consequently, I have to admit that I admire Moustakas's daring effort to take on the unenviable task of trying to understand human experience in the most direct manner without appealing to the many objectivistic methods of which he was undoubtedly aware. He knew that a more direct, penetrating procedure was called for, and he developed first his heuristic mode of inquiry and then his mode of phenomenological analysis. If I direct some critical comments toward some of his methodical expressions, it is only to strengthen the very phenomenological approach he adopted. Had Moustakas outlived me, I'm sure that he would have brought critical comments to my applications of phenomenology in his typically kind way. In any case, I would not complain, especially if his comments helped strengthen phenomenological applications to psychology, a goal we both shared.

²   Moustakas's (1967) article on heuristic research also appeared in a collection edited by James Bugental. It is identical to the chapter that appears in Moustakas's book *Individuality and Encounter*, which I used for my commentary and which was published in 1968. I stated that this was the first time Moustakas articulated what he meant by heuristic research. Because the date is later than its appearance in the Bugental collection, it may seem as though there was an earlier expression of his method. However, since the same article appears in both places, I have to assume that it was only written once but submitted to both books. The fact that *Individuality and Encounter* has a 1968 publication date rather than 1967, which is the date Bugental's collection came out, I attribute to publication lag.

³ After I came across this article and saw that the detailed description of a phenomenological method looked suspiciously similar to the way I had articulated the phenomenological method as applied to psychology, I emailed Bruce Douglass (early June, 2015) and asked for the source from which he got his information. I also told him that I had a vague memory that there was another article by him and Moustakas explicitly mentioning that my version of the phenomenological method was used to contrast how heuristic inquiry differed from phenomenology. I asked Douglass if my memory was correct and, if it was, to please send me the appropriate reference. I also told him that if it was easier for him, he could simply send me a list of his publications and I would pursue the matter myself. Douglass did respond and confirmed that the method I articulated was one of the phenomenological methods, along with Keen's, that they had used. But he was not able to identify the article from which the application of phenomenology to psychology was drawn.

[4] I was aware of Keen's manuscript but wasn't sure how to get a copy. I contacted the Simon Silverman Phenomenology Center located in the Duquesne University Library, which fortunately had a copy. I would like to thank the Silverman Center for allowing me to use their copy so that I could check for myself what Keen said about texture and structure.

# Chapter 4
## An Example of the Application of Phenomenology in Psychological Research

Earlier, I (Giorgi, 1985, 2009) had developed a method for the analysis of psychological data based on the philosophical phenomenological method that Husserl (1983) had developed. I used some insights from Merleau-Ponty's (1962) articulation of Husserl's philosophical method as well. I had reasoned at that time that since Husserl had already developed a phenomenological method, it seemed logical to simply adapt it for psychological purposes instead of starting from scratch to come up with a scientific version of that method. After studying phenomenological philosophy for several years, I realized that basing psychology on phenomenological philosophy rather than on empiricism would be greatly beneficial for the discipline of psychology. But I also realized that in order for phenomenology to have an impact on psychology some type of praxis would have to be established. It simply would not do to merely present another theoretical perspective. Psychology was already replete with theories, and all of its facts were empirically based. Phenomenological philosophy was suggesting a radically different orientation for the gathering of facts and their meanings. Thus, I thought that it was critical to establish a method for determining and analyzing psychological data from a phenomenological perspective. However, phenomenological philosophy is so rich that I never doubted that a family of methods could be derived from it—not just a single method.

When one begins to study phenomenology, one quickly discovers the importance of the notion of intentionality. Many acts of consciousness are directed toward objects, whether these objects are intrinsic to consciousness or external to it and whether the objects actually exist or not. This orientation of acts of consciousness to objects is what defines intentionality. While intentionality itself is not essential to consciousness, it is essential for consciousness to have acts that do partake of intentionality. It is a key factor in our understanding of the world. While the discovery of intentionality (Brentano, 1973) preceded phenomenology, it was with Husserl that intentionality was developed and refined and became a cornerstone of phenomenological analyses. We psychologists need to remember that intentionality was discovered within a philosophical context and that it is basically a philosophical term. Yet, it is so critical to the understanding of consciousness that one can hardly do without it if one is to understand conscious, experiential, or even behavioral phenomena. How then is one to put intentionality to good use if one is not a philosopher? More specifically, how can psychologists use intentionality for psychological rather than philosophical purposes?

I don't know anyone who has defined very precisely the dividing line between philosophical and psychological analyses, although there are concrete analyses that are clearly philosophical and others that are clearly psychological. I would say that Husserl is always philosophical and van den Berg always psychological. But where does Merleau-Ponty fall? It seems that the philosopher of ambiguity is, appropriately enough, ambiguous with respect to that dividing line, especially when he deals with psychological themes. Yet no one would deny that his analyses are sharp and clarifying with respect to the problems he undertakes. Fortunately, I do not want to deal with dividing line issues; rather, I want to try to understand how a schema drawn from phenomenological philosophy can be helpful when applied to concrete psychological data. While, the schema itself is actually universal with respect to human functioning, how it is applied to the concrete, particular subjective experience of an individual in order to derive psychological findings is as yet undetermined. The critical question is: Can we apply the schema as such, or must it be modified in some way?

When I first went to Duquesne University in the early 1960s, Adrian van Kaam was the leading theoretician, and he was constantly introducing phenomenological terms into psychology. In those early years van Kaam (1966, p. 53) defined psychology as the study of the intentional–functional behavior of individuals. He thought that expression essentially defined the common object of study for psychology. My own background was in "positivistic–empirical psychology" and, at the time, I was overwhelmed by so many new terms coming from existential phenomenology that I barely had time to sort them out. I noticed his definition, and while I thought that it was a good start, it somehow seemed to me incomplete. However, I was busy with many issues, including the task of developing a phenomenological method for psychology, so I let the matter rest. Recently, a half century later, I have come back to his definition to see if I could make it viable. I have in fact reworked it. I want to explore if the resulting modified schema that follows can be the foundation for another type of phenomenological psychological analysis.

## A Phenomenological Schema

While I think van Kaam's idea that psychology consists of studying the intentional–functional relations humans have with the world is a good start for conducting phenomenological psychological analyses, I also think that the expression is not quite adequate as it stands. It is too brief, too truncated to do justice to most phenomena because it leaves out the awareness of the "given." If one starts behaving, one cannot discount the situation of which consciousness is aware and toward which the acts are directed. What is presented to consciousness modifies the functioning because it is a kind of feedback with respect to the goal of the actor. In other words, one has to take into account the fulfilling aspects (or their lack) of the intentional effort. Consequently, the schema gets more complicated and looks like this:

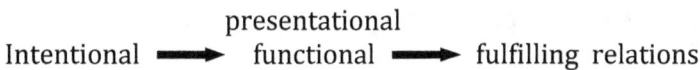

$$\text{Intentional} \longrightarrow \begin{array}{c} \text{presentational} \\ \text{functional} \end{array} \longrightarrow \text{fulfilling relations}$$

The revised schema then indicates that there are relationships between intentional and presentational features as well as between intentional and functional features and between presentational and fulfilling aspects and functional and fulfilling aspects. There are also relations between the presentational and functional features. In other words, the schema is vividly dynamic. It should also be noted that the schema as presented above is basically a cognitive schema. It does not reflect conative and affective factors that also influence the experiential process, although affective factors can impact the analysis guided by the above cognitive schema when they are present in the raw data. The question I shall try to answer here is: Can one make practical use of this schema for research purposes, or is it hopelessly cumbersome? I believe that the schema can be useful, and I shall attempt to apply it in this article.

## Research on the Psychology of Learning

I have many examples of descriptions of learning because it is a field that I have researched quite a bit. Phenomenology is not in principle against quantification, but it begins research with a qualitative perspective and will utilize quantification only if a relevant quantitative question spontaneously presents itself. Consequently, the typical point of departure in phenomenological psychological research is to obtain a description of a concrete experience of the phenomenon being researched. In the description I am about to present, the participant (P), at the time of her description, intends to convey to the researcher an incident that she believes is an adequate response to the researcher's question, which was: "Please describe for me a situation in which you experienced learning." Obviously, P directed herself to a particular incident, presumably one of many from her past, and she describes how the learning situation unfolded for her. So her description is a memorial one, but once having noted that fact we are inside the selected situation. The language of the description is in the past tense, and everything that is described is how the event took place according to her perception of it. In other words, P is presenting a phenomenal depiction of her experience and her description takes place within the natural attitude.

### Description of Learning from within the Natural Attitude
Here is the raw data as provided by P:

> During August I spent ten days in San Francisco, staying with a couple I had not met before. They were friends of the person I was traveling with. Both of these people are professionals, busy in their respective occupations. They were also caring for the two-and-a-half- year-old son of the man. During our stay, Harry and Ann (not real names) gave us the use of one of their cars and urged us to enjoy ourselves in the city. They shopped, cooked, cleaned, and also worked. My friend and I took care of our own possessions, trying to interfere as little as possible with the rhythm of the home. I offered throughout the first three days of our stay to help with the maintenance chores, and each offer was politely refused. The five of us were also sharing lots of play time together.
>
> I began to feel uncomfortable with not contributing more to the process of meeting the needs of all of us in the house. I talked with my traveling companion about my discomfort, and he

reassured me, saying that Harry and Ann would ask if/when they wanted help. I still felt that Harry and Ann really did want assistance, and that they were not asking for it. I was experiencing some awkwardness with just going ahead and doing things in the kitchen, etc., as I was afraid of messing up plans for meals or being too forward in any way. I was also afraid to check out my suspicions with Harry and Ann directly, because they appeared to be at ease with what was happening. I continued to offer assistance, and the refusals continued also.

The evening of the fifth day of our stay, my friend and I came back from a day in the city. Harry and Ann were painting their kitchen. As I walked in the house and saw them, I felt the fear and awkwardness around actually assisting in some way come over me again. I went into the living room, frustrated that the good feelings of the day were dissipating. My friend came in and sat down with me, asking me what was wrong. I explained that I wanted to help but that I felt sure my offer would be refused. My friend asked me if I really did want to help. I started thinking, "Yes I do, I would enjoy helping." I realized that my offers had been made timidly, that I had been feeling like a guest and offering to help as if I didn't really have much to offer. I reviewed mentally my approaches to Harry and Ann in the last few days, and realized that I had been expecting refusals from the beginning. I thought that in my own home, I'm more likely to refuse help from a guest or not ask for it even when I wanted it. Still, inside, I felt very positive about working with them to create an easier time with more sharing for us all, and I decided that I had been inhibiting myself out of fear instead of stating what I wanted. I went into the kitchen and said that I wanted to help cook dinner. Harry heard me, and I felt that this was because I had made a positive statement. I learned that in this situation I had definite personal wants that I could state, and that I had been inhibiting myself by judging what their judgment would be in advance.

## Analysis of Data

We are now going to apply the above-mentioned schema to the raw data presented by P. The schema is considered to be a universal depiction of the key constituents of the structure of experiencing from a phenomenological cognitive perspective. We have to look and see what happens to the relationships among the constituents when learning takes place and then see if we can essentialize those relationships. We grant that the structure comes from phenomenological philosophy, but we look for the psychological implications when we apply the structure. The first step is to read the entire description in order to get a sense of the whole. A phenomenological analysis should not begin without some idea of how the description proceeds and ends.

However, it should be kept in mind that the reading of the raw data has to take place within the attitude of what I call the "scientific phenomenological reduction" and Husserl (1977) calls the "phenomenological psychological reduction." This attitude is not, of course, the transcendental phenomenological reduction, but Husserl allowed that a psychological reduction could take place, and with the latter reduction the intentional objects of any act are reduced, although the acts themselves are considered to be human acts. Consequently, we can claim that the acts do belong to existing humans, and thus the findings of the analysis can be applied to humans in general even if the objects referred to are only considered to be the way the objects or situations presented themselves to the experiencer without the additional claim that they actually existed the way they were given in their presentations. Thus, when P stated that she felt her hosts really desired some help with their chores, we claim that was the way P perceived the situation, without claiming that was the way it actually was. In other words, the learning situation as described by P is a completely experiential one. It tells us how everything appeared to and was interpreted by P, and there is no reference to objective reality.

The second step requires the researcher to go back to the beginning of the description and look for tensions in the "intentional-presentational/functional-fulfilling" relations. As one reads through the first paragraph. one sees that what is expressed there are mostly intentional-presentational-fulfilling relationships that do not require much functioning from P. What is presented to P is the "busy-ness" and work that the host couple is performing, and P perceives that there is a certain rhythm to all that they do. P notes that she and her friend, as guests, wanted to respect that rhythm and not interfere with it when they took care of their own chores. P also perceived that the hosts were being generous to their guests. If one switched the penultimate and last sentences of the first paragraph in P's description, then one could say that the whole paragraph reveals no serious tensions, except for the newly designated last sentence (I offered throughout the first three days of our stay to help with the maintenance chores, and each offer was politely refused). The newly designated last sentence reveals a mildly expressed discordant tone. It indicates that P perceives that a lot of work is being done by the hosts, for themselves of course, but also for their guests. Thus, P feels obliged to offer to be of help in some way and, in fact, does offer her services to her hosts, but her offer is politely declined. One could say that the arousal of a sense of obligation on the part of P is a call for a certain type of functioning in response to what was being presented to her. In other words, P experiences a certain lack of fulfillment with respect to functioning and therefore is left with a certain vaguely felt need.

In the second paragraph, P begins by acknowledging her discomfort because her offer to assist her hosts with their chores was declined. Because of the "busy-ness" of the hosts' lives, P perceives that they could use help, especially since she as a guest was a beneficiary of their efforts, but her offers to help were always declined. This inability to function in accord with what was being presented to her perceptually introduced a certain tension in her experience. The harmonious relationship among all of the constituents of her experience was beginning to break down. In fact, the tension related to her inability to function in accord with her perceptions was felt strongly enough by P for her to turn to her friend, who was more familiar with the hosts, to seek his advice. Her friend's advice was reassuring to P. He told her that if their hosts needed or wanted help, they would communicate that idea to her. P, however, for some reason perceived that the hosts really wanted some help but were not asking for it. This left P with a presentational situation that had some tension built into it: P perceives that the hosts not only could use some help, but even preferred it; however, when she offers to help, her offers are declined. The idea of simply going ahead and helping her hosts occurred to P, but she was afraid that such direct action might make her appear forward, and that would have been socially awkward for her. She was also afraid to confirm whether or not her suspicion that her hosts really wanted help was correct because to P they seemed to be comfortable with what was going on. This makes one wonder where P got the notion that the hosts were desirous of help. But whatever its source, it created a tension in the eidetic structure that consisted of the presentational-functioning-fulfilling relationships.

The third and last paragraph details many of the dynamics that were being lived by P in the situation she described. By this time, we have arrived at the fifth day of her stay, and P states that they came home from a visit to the city feeling good. But as soon as P perceived that the hosts were painting their kitchen, she once again experienced feelings of "fear and awkwardness" come over her, replacing the good feelings that were engendered by her visit to the city. Apparently, her mood shift was visible enough for her friend to notice, and he asked her if something was troubling her. P explained to her friend that she wanted to help the hosts with their chores but was afraid that her offer would be refused again. Her friend asked her if she really wanted to help. This question provoked some deeper thinking in P. P somehow became aware that she did entertain a genuine desire to help but that her offers were being made timidly, and in a polite, socially acceptable way—from the perspective of a guest. The role of being a guest had certain implicit meanings for P, of which she was only just then becoming aware. P caught herself responding in her role as a guest as she would have desired a guest to behave if she were the hostess. P knew that as a hostess she would refuse help from a guest who volunteered to help her and would do so even if she wanted some help. Apparently, the meaning of host–guest relationship assumed by P was not being lived by her hosts. P came to the realization that in her assumed role as guest, which she apparently automatically accepted on the basis of past experience, she was behaving in a polite manner, i.e., in a socially prescribed way of behaving. Thus, she was not expressing herself in a genuinely authentic way—a way that would make manifest what she really desired. Realizing all this, P says that she went into the kitchen and assertively stated that she wanted to help cook dinner. She perceived that the host heard her and spontaneously accepted her offer. P concluded she learned that she had deep personal wants that she could correctly express to others, but that she had been inhibiting herself because she posited that the judgment of others would be non-accepting even before she pronounced her intention. She also became aware that she should not limit herself to socially prescribed roles when a more authentic communication was called for.

In P's description of learning, what was primarily given was a discrepancy between what was being presented to P and the functioning that she believed that she was allowed to carry out. Her perception indicated that her busy hosts could use help—especially since in the midst of their own busy lives they were extending themselves to be helpful to their guests (which included P). And P was aware that she was a relatively new acquaintance who was the beneficiary of good deeds and warm acceptance mostly due to her relationship with her traveling friend. In other words, the presentational-functional relationship was not fully harmonious, and so P did not experience complete fulfillment. The lack of complete fulfillment, while possibly discounted in the early part of her stay, weighed upon her sufficiently over time so that eventually she had to recognize it because it became troubling. The generosity of her hosts continued, and when they undertook an especially arduous task (painting their kitchen) P could no longer tolerate her uneasiness. One could say that an emotional moment interrupts the presentational-functional schema in such a way that the lack of proper functioning can no longer be tolerated by P. At that moment, a certain goal announces itself to P, and the desire to be helpful becomes her primary ambition. But how? She had offered to help several times and she was always turned down. At this key moment, help comes from her significant other. He notices that she is upset and asks her why she appears to be troubled. As she explains her dilemma to him—the fact that she wants to help out but that the hosts won't let her—she begins to become aware of her manner of offering to help. She realizes that her mode of offering was socially polite—a mode of offering that she herself rejects when she is a hostess—and because of that, it lacked conviction. Consequently, challenged by her friend, P first acknowledges to herself that she really desires to be helpful and then convincingly announces to her hosts that she is going to help with dinner and sees that her offer is readily accepted. The gap between what was presented to her awareness and how to respond with proper functioning was closed, and fulfillment was experienced.

**Reflection on the Analysis**
In the above example, learning was required in order to resolve the difference between the demands of what was presented to P and the proper way of responding to those demands so that fulfillment could be experienced. However, the schema we employed does not speak directly to the phenomenon of learning. It is too general to be specifically enlightening with respect to learning. The schema can tell us that there is a problem in the presentational-functional relationship, but not necessarily what the problem is or how to resolve it. One can imagine that different specific experiences might have different ways of resolving the experiential problems being depicted, but since the current description was produced in response to a request for an experience of learning, it's not surprising that learning was involved to resolve the problematic issue. The key methodological point here is that I had to depart from the general schema being tested in order to clarify all the issues presented in the description. The schema was helpful in

detecting the location of the problem and perhaps in detailing something of the nature of the problem, but it did not really speak to the question of resolving the problem. If this schema is to be employed in the analysis of experiential descriptions, unless I am missing something very important, it will have to be supplemented by other phenomenological experiential methods. The focus of the generic method does not allow the details of the solution to announce themselves.

## A Complementary Analysis

The original description provided us with the problem the experiencer was having along with the solution to the problem. The general schema we employed above was able to pinpoint the problem from a phenomenological perspective, but it was not helpful when it came to an analysis of the solution. One reason is that the method has a precommitment to specifying presentational-functional-fulfilling relationships, and if the solution is not articulated in terms of those relationships then the method cannot focus on the details of the solution. In order for a method to be able to analyze a whole description regardless of its content, it has to be more open-ended. Consequently, I (Giorgi, 2009) applied the method I had previously developed to the part of the description that told us the way that P solved her problem.

The scientific phenomenological method actually requires that one demarcate the raw data into meaning units; however, since the part of the description that presents the solution of the problem is brief, we can consider each paragraph to be a meaning unit. Consequently, in turning to the raw data, my attitude, while still in the scientific phenomenological reduction mode, had to take on a more specific focus, and thus examine the raw data for aspects of the description that might throw light on the phenomenon of learning. Thus, I am looking for aspects of the description that would be relevant for the experience of learning, even though I don't posit explicit criteria for the phenomenon of learning. The attitude employed is more like the attitude Merleau-Ponty (1962, p. 28) described as one of "circumscribed ignorance," an attitude that has an "empty" but "already determinate intention," which is what attention is. It has to be appreciated that the method being employed is a "discovery-oriented" method and not a "hypothesis-verifying" one. When using the latter type of method, the criteria have to be explicit because one has to know which criteria are being used to make the claim that something is indeed true. But it is different with a discovery-oriented method.

With a discovery-oriented method, especially one involving morphological phenomena, new insights into the very criteria being used are possible. (Morphological phenomena are descriptively based phenomena with irregular dimensions that cannot be fully determined by formal implications.) The lack of an initial explicit statement of criteria also allows the researcher to tap into prepredicative levels of functioning (Husserl, 1973) or indeterminate zones of experiencing (Merleau-Ponty, 1962) whence new aspects of the objects of experiencing can be encountered. The method is not an intellectualistic one, but an existential or embodied one. After all, not everything is already known, and space must be left for the new to announce itself; maximum openness is necessary for that to happen. This is especially important for prelogical or pararational phenomena, categories within which most psychological phenomena reside. Eventually, criteria are posited, but that happens within the context of the analysis. In order to appreciate what the method achieves, I must articulate some aspects of phenomenological philosophy, which in turn is the basis of a phenomenological theory of science. The differences with empirically based methods are profound because of the richer and deeper understanding of consciousness provided by phenomenology.

The insights of Merleau-Ponty and Husserl converge rather nicely to help us articulate the dimensions of experiencing that lie behind the steps of the method. A key point that has to be appreciated is that attention also explores a preobjective world wherein indeterminate objects dwell. Merleau-Ponty's (1962, p. 28) criticism of "empirical-intellectualistic" theories of perception is that they all presuppose a completed, objective, determinate world. His critique demonstrates forcefully that in the traditional views "Perceptual consciousness is confused with the exact forms of scientific consciousness and the indeterminate does not enter into the definition of mind." This view leaves consciousness without any work to do. However, careful descriptions show that consciousness in its mode of being attentive is tremendously active. As Merleau-Ponty (1962) states,

> To pay attention is not merely further to elucidate pre-existing data, it is to bring about a new articulation of them by taking them as figures. They are preformed only as horizons, they constitute in reality new regions in the total world....(Attention is) but the active constitution of a new object which makes explicit and articulate what was until then presented as no more than an indeterminate horizon....It gives rise to the

'knowledge-bringing event', which is to transform it, only by means of the still ambiguous meaning which it requires that event to clarify; it is therefore the motive and not the cause of the event. (pp. 30–31)

Consciousness can do its work only if one does not assume that the world is complete and fully determined. There is a secondary attention, "which is limited to recalling knowledge already gained" (Merleau-Pony, 1962, p. 30), but that type of functioning does not exhaust the powers of consciousness. It has to be appreciated that consciousness functioning in its attentive mode can be "a change in the structure of consciousness, the establishment of a new dimension of experience, the setting forth of an a priori" (Merleau-Ponty, 1962, p. 30; italics in original). This means that a certain ability is established—an ability to perceive phenomena that were not possible before the work of consciousness and the establishment of a new a priori.

It has to be appreciated that when one is exploring the phenomenal realm it is not the same as when one explores objective reality. The concrete experiencing of the perceptual realm dealing with experiential phenomena cannot be forced into the categories of objectivity. Merleau-Ponty (1962) has convincingly argued that "a complete reform of understanding is called for if we are to translate phenomena accurately" (p. 49). He continues to emphasize that

the perception of our own body and the perception of external things provide an example of *non-positing* consciousness, that is, of consciousness not in possession of fully determinate objects, that of a *logic lived through* which cannot account for itself, and that of an *immanent meaning* which is not clear to itself.... (p. 49, italics in original)

It takes supplementary experiencing to bring about clarity. That is why the criteria cannot be posited beforehand. They have to emerge from the analytic process. To understand phenomena as lived, a break has to be made with the categories of objectivity and realism. One has to track the dynamics of the functioning of consciousness and describe carefully how the acts of consciousness in its attentive mode transform the mental field and exhibit "a new way for consciousness to be present to its objects" (Merleau-Ponty, 1962, p. 29).

Husserl also found it necessary to foray beyond the objective world. As a logician he was interested in propositions and predicative sentences, so he realized that he had to explore the prepredicative realm in order to understand acts of predication more fully. His descriptions of that world are complex and intricate. Thus, we will only give a broad summary of how he views the process of predication, which should be sufficient for the purposes of this article. Husserl's (1973) analyses are primarily contained in *Experience and Judgment*, but Moneta (1972) has also written a succinct and reliable account of his theory of predication.

In broad steps, Husserl's (1973; Moneta, 1972) understanding of predication is as follows: "Husserl maintains that the predicative activity of consciousness is rooted in, and to that extent derived from, the prepredicative sphere. At the same time, however, the activity of predication is 'originary' activity in the sense that it is productive of a categorial object" (Moneta, 1972, p. 171). At the prepredicative level of experiencing, Husserl (1973) observes that there is only passive data, i.e., "a field of determinate structure, one of prominences and articulated particularities" (p. 72). This field can only be established abstractly, and Husserl (1973) makes clear that "it is not yet a field of objectivities in the true sense of the term (because )...an object is the product of an objectivating operation of the ego and...an operation of predicative judgment" (p. 72). The noticing of "prominences and particularities" falls far short of such objectivating procedures. Included in the prepredicative experience is an awareness of the world horizon, which "is not an object of experience,...rather a presence, lived in the form of implicit awareness of the world (which means) that aspect of the life of consciousness which functions in a hidden and anonymous way" (Moneta, 1972, p. 172). To shed some light on the hidden function of consciousness, one has to clarify the intentional sense of the objects of experience, which are always individual objects, and the clarification of the sense of the objects depends upon how they present themselves. As Moneta (1972) says, "The 'how' is the access to the 'that'" (p. 175).

Because the horizonal structure of the world includes belief in the world, Husserl identifies prepredicative experience with perceptual experience. This perceptual presence to the object takes place before predication itself begins. It is an extremely rudimentary kind of perception that lacks full attention to or full engagement with the object. It is a fundamentally receptive experience, but for Husserl even receptivity implies a minimum of activity. This rudimentary perception is transformed when the ego produces acts which "hold-in-grasp" or "maintain-in-grasp" the object that was minimally noticed, and when the ego is involved, the "holding-in-grasp" actualized is different from its employment in simple apprehension (Husserl, 1973, p. 118). The series of acts that "maintain-the-object-in-grasp" allow time for the explication of the object, and thus the sense of the object is altered. "The perceived object has now become the subject of predicable properties" (Moneta, 1972, p. 179), and therefore it has accrued multiple determinations. The new determinations themselves do not arise from the prepredicative sphere but are produced by means of conscious acts. The ultimate goal is the "once-for-all determination" of the object that is present to consciousness (Husserl, 1973, p. 198).

Thus, both Merleau-Ponty and Husserl demonstrate that one has to go beyond or, perhaps more accurately, below, objectivity in order to understand how objectivity is constituted. One has to encounter the indeterminate level of experiencing and track the process whereby determinations occur. The achievement of this task necessitates the exploration of how conscious acts function, which in turn requires careful reflection and description. We will now see that the application of the psychological phenomenological method requires many of the same processes that Merleau-Ponty and Husserl described. These processes apply to both the discovery of psychological dimensions of experiencing and the constituents of learning.

### The Process of Applying the Scientific Phenomenological Method to Psychological Data

Of course, one analyzes the data from within the perspective of the scientific phenomenological reduction. Along with the former perspective, one examines the raw data with the "circumscribed ignorant or indeterminate" attitude, which creates a certain tension hovering around the seeking of "psychological dimensions relevant for learning." The reader will note the complexity of this attitude. Both the meaning of psychology and the meaning of learning are left open-ended. Let me deal with psychology first.

It is pretty well understood by most psychologists that the precise and genuine meaning of psychology is not yet an historical achievement. It is often the case that sciences exist before a clarified understanding of their nature can be made explicit. There are certainly definitions aplenty—the science of behavior or consciousness or experience or even of the unconscious. But each of these terms still leave ambiguities. The terms are too broad because there is, for example, political behavior, historical consciousness, artistic experience, and unconscious social identities. Moreover, if each term is partially correct, how does one integrate the four of them? Probably most psychologists are guided by some covert meaning of the term, and the best way to discover the actual meanings being used is to let that meaning express itself. Allow it to become manifest in the living of a psychological analysis. That is what the phenomenological discovery method allows one to do. An inspection of the analysis may determine the actual way the term was used. From a phenomenological perspective, a psychological analysis means detecting the individuated lived meanings contained in concrete experiences. This definition can undoubtedly be made more precise, but at least it delimits the field somewhat.

I am also guided by an understanding of learning, which is not made explicit; the openness thus provided also allows for new dimensions of experiences relevant for learning to appear. So, let me try to describe how this process works by returning to the analysis of the raw data already performed. If we return to the last paragraph of P's description, we see that P was feeling good after returning from a day in the city but reported that the good feeling dissipated as soon as she perceived that her hosts were painting their kitchen. Admittedly, this seems to be a rather extreme activity while hosting guests, but there it was, and P's perception of it precipitated in her feelings of "fear and awkwardness." When reading this within my research attitude, I hesitate and pause. I ask myself, are these feelings themselves constituents of learning? I think not. But might they be relevant for learning in this particular example? Yes, I think so. After all, it was "feelings of uncomfortableness" surrounding the denials of her offers to help that introduced tensions in the presentational-functional-fulfilling relations that P was living. I become aware that feelings are playing a role in the totality of this experience, and a place must be made for them. So I tentatively distinguish between the context of learning and learning per se. Perhaps her awkward feelings belong to the context of learning. I will have to see how this distinction will hold up.

But I'm also doing an analysis from a psychological perspective. From that perspective, feelings are surely important for they tell us how things are going for us with others and the world. P is expressing feelings of awkwardness, which tells us that somehow things are not going smoothly for her either with others or in her world or both.

I come back to P's feelings of awkwardness. For P, the most direct way for her to alleviate those feelings would be for her to help her hosts with their chores. But that direct route was blocked. Her offers are declined. P is still not aware of how to solve her problem, but she is aware of her negative feelings and seems concerned about them.

Apparently, her distress is sufficiently visible for her partner to notice because he asks her if something is wrong. I note that the negative feelings are playing a significant role in this experience. If they are not learning per se, they certainly have to be given some role in the whole experience. After all, because of those negative feelings, a significant other intervenes in a caring way and P interrogates a personal experiential process that obviously has a public dimension. P then explains her dilemma to her partner—that she wants to help their hosts but her offers of help are turned down. And for reasons that are unclear to us, he asks her if she really wants to help.

Certain speculations are possible here: Maybe her partner was perceiving that P's offers were made timidly or in such a way that they were satisfying a merely superficial, social demand. Or knowing P fairly well, he is aware that she really does not like to work too hard. Or whatever! The point is that the method does not allow one to indulge in such speculations because speculations become interpretations, and the method is descriptive, not interpretive. The researcher has to stick with solidly established, intuited, lived meanings as determined by a psychological perspective concentrating on the phenomenon of learning. We only know that her partner asked P if she really wanted to help, but we do not know why he asked her that particular question. We can, however, ascertain that that question was highly relevant for the manifestation of learning because it provoked some deeper thinking in P. It's as though before that point she was completely unaware of how she was offering to be helpful to her hosts. Perhaps the question caught her by surprise; but, in any case, we know that she began reflecting on the manner in which she was offering to be helpful. Her reflection indicated to her that perhaps she was not expressing herself as fully as she was feeling.

I note to myself here that this insight could be designated as something she learned about herself, and perhaps is a part of the actual learning that took place in the stricter sense as opposed to being part of learning's context. With this insight, I confirm that making discoveries about self or the world can belong to the phenomenon of learning. I do not say that it exhausts learning or that more might not be needed. But whatever the ultimate meaning of learning turns out to be, a sense of discovery at least belongs to a type of it. A quick, imaginative variation of other ways that discoveries can belong to the experience of learning confirms this insight.

We should also note the context within which the discovery occurred to her. It took place against an awakened experiential history. P had written, "I realized that my offers had been made timidly, that I had been feeling like a guest....I reviewed mentally my approaches to Harry and Ann in the last few days, and realized that I had been expecting refusals from the beginning. I thought that in my own home, I'm more likely to refuse help from a guest or not ask for it even when I wanted it." P thus discovers that she was treating this new situation according to how she lived similar situations in the past. But her feelings of awkwardness regarding her hosts' refusals of help announced to her that somehow she was not living this situation as smoothly as in the past. Her partner's questioning of her motivation perhaps also surprised her. In any case, because the way she was living her situation was at odds with what she desired awakened her to the fact that perhaps something was amiss. She started reflecting on what was happening and realized that her genuine feelings regarding the desire to help her hosts were not being revealed in her modes of expression. Or better, she discovered that her modes of expressing her desire to be helpful to her hosts were being determined more by situational expectations or habitual modes of expression rather than by the genuine desire to be helpful that she discovered she was feeling.

However, in addition to discovering that her mode of asking for help was deficient, P also had to imagine a more authentic way of expressing her desire to help. This involved some risk. There was still the question of whether she could pull it off. Learning in this situation is not only the discovery on P's part that she was responding politely and habitually to a situation that called for a more authentic, felt response, but there was also an element of incertitude concerning her ability to act or speak in a way that would be acceptable to her hosts. Neither the risk nor any doubts concerning success of her new-found strategy are mentioned by P. Nevertheless, they belong to the situation because they are possibilities that cannot be eliminated. By considering such possibilities, the phenomenological analysis can bring to light relevant factors not explicitly mentioned by the describer.

In any case, P decided to act according to her newly discovered deeper desire to be helpful, and she knew that she was successful because her host accepted her pronouncement that she was going to help, along with her actions. Thus, the sense of learning in this situation is deepened by her action because P not only discovered some deep feelings that were previously hidden but was also able to act in a manner that was consistent with these feelings;   furthermore, her message clearly had been accepted by the hosts, who had been previously indifferent to her offers. The learning process therefore involved (1) the discovery of feelings that were more in line with her situation, (2) a correct interpretation of what the feelings urged her to do, and (3) the ability to act on those feelings and have her actions and intentions accepted by her hosts.

But there is one thing lacking for the most robust sense of learning: Can she repeat this process again? The sense of learning implies a certain generality, the idea that what was once achieved can be repeated. In this description there is only a hint that P may be able to repeat what she achieved in this situation when she said, "I learned that in this situation I had definite personal wants that I could state...." But there is no evidence that she actually accomplished such a task again. So the description serves as an example of how a learned behavior may initiate and develop but stops short of being a robust example of learning. Still, it is insightful with respect to the beginnings of a type of learning process and with the dynamics of achieving a successful outcome.

At this point in the research process, I'd like to point out how the phenomenological concepts articulated by Husserl and Merleau-Ponty and presented above have played a role in the analytic process. Obviously, I cannot cover the whole process in an article of this length, but perhaps some indicators will help. While I stated that I did not posit explicit criteria, which allowed me to remain open to aspects of the experience I might have otherwise avoided, I did nevertheless consider criteria when specific moments of the data had to be considered. Thus, P's "feelings of awkwardness" when returning home and observing her hosts painting their kitchen made me pause. Those feelings announce themselves as important, but what is their role for the phenomenon of learning? Because I am now in a phenomenological psychological perspective (whereas P's description was from a natural attitude Lifeworld perspective), I have a different angle on what she said. I now see the feelings precipitating an experiential process that will result in learning for P. A certain whole, connected by motivational relationships or meaningful implications, starts to stand out. I make the effort to produce the whole: awkward feelings, thwarted desire to help hosts, P's annoyance visible to partner, partner inquires about P's feelings, P expresses her desire to help but doesn't know how, partner asks if she really wants to help, P interrogates her feelings, P differentiates present situation from similar ones in her past, P discovers that her mode of offering is not commensurate with her feelings, P risks new mode of offering without guarantee of success, P sees that her offer is accepted.

Assuming a psychological perspective provides a new articulation of the data and helps create a new a priori. The new a priori is the psychological relationships among the meanings, not their Lifeworld relationships. What was indeterminate or perhaps vague from the Lifeworld perspective is now determinate because of the motivational relationships the psychological perspective uncovered. The feelings of awkwardness precipitated a process that resulted in a transformation of P's situation for the better. She was failing to achieve what she desired but ended up doing precisely what she desired because she managed to perform a proper response. A more complete analysis would also show that what P was desiring would have to be understood as a categorial object. We could say that P thought, "I desire to help my generous hosts with their chores because of the kind way they have treated me." This is a complex goal requiring non-sensorial contributions of consciousness, but it would take us too far afield to fully articulate all the implications of that statement. Overall, the phenomenological psychological approach tries to uncover the intricate and complex role of consciousness in our everyday experiencing. It is too often passed over in contemporary psychological analyses. With the transcendental phenomenological reduction, one discovers that subjectivity is a meaning-constituting entity. With the scientific phenomenological reduction (Husserl's phenomenological psychological reduction), one discovers the individual meanings that a human consciousness can constitute in situations of the Lifeworld.

The last step of the method requires one to review the whole process and to make hard decisions with respect to the outcomes that one wants to defend. I will start with the structure of this particular experience and then indicate how I would back it up. The structure about to be described is a type of one-time learning achievement, and not at all universal, but it has been raised to an eidetic level with the help of imaginative variation. The structure is: *For P, a one-time learning experience involves the discovery—with the help of discordant feelings and with the help of another—that one's modes of expression to others have to be based on authentic feelings rather than on more habitual-superficial modes of expression; furthermore, the expressed communications have to be backed by appropriate actions that are accepted by relevant others.* While this structure reflects the specificity of P's situation, mostly because it is based on a single description, it is nevertheless expressed in such a way that one can easily imagine others living this same structure in different situations. For example, a student expressing a minority viewpoint to a class after his teacher has instructed and encouraged him to tell the audience what he really feels, would also fall under the structure. (In standard research situations, of course, more than one participant would be used, which complicates the getting of the structure but does not change the overall strategy.)

The last step of the method demands that one review the structure in order to achieve final confirmation of the results. It starts by saying that "For P, a one-time learning experience...." The qualification that it is a one-time learning experience holds up because, as we discussed, there is no strong evidence that P was able to act on her genuine feelings again. There is a hint, but that is not sufficient. A second constituent is "a discovery that one's modes of expressions to others have to be based upon authentic feelings rather than habitual-superficial modes of expression." Critical for learning in this context is that the need for authentic expression is a discovery. If the authentic expression were to be spontaneously produced, it would simply be a correct performance. But for the occurrence of learning there had to be a problem for which the authentic expression was a solution. The problem was lived interpersonally between P and her partner and between P and her hosts. The fact that something was not quite right was announced to P by her "awkward and fearful feelings," and so I add a sense of "discordant feelings" as another constituent to the structure because I think that the feelings were important for the discovery to take place. However, eidetically I wanted a more general depiction of the feelings because it is easy to imagine that some other feelings (e.g., anger) could have provoked her self-interrogation. But the awakened feelings would have to be out of harmony with all that was going on. Hence, I use the term "discordant" to convey the idea that the feelings have to be disharmonious with her actions. Here is how the essential and the empirical are related in phenomenological research: It is essential that some sense of discordant feeling be present to alert the subject that she is not at peace with all that is going on, but the fact that it is "awkwardness and fear" is an empirical variation rather than an essential factor.

I have added, "with the help of another" as a constituent. This might be problematic for some researchers. Can I imagine that someone may discover that he or she has to express him- or herself authentically on one's own? Perhaps. But our perspective is also psychological. And when the partner asked P if she really wanted to help, I think that it made P interrogate herself in a significantly different way. There was a special challenge to his question that provoked a type of self-reflection that may have been missing if she merely wondered on her own why she was having difficulties. That intuition presents itself to me strongly, so I will include it as a constituent. Future research may indicate that I am wrong, in which case I will modify the structure.

The final constituent is "expressed communications have to be backed by appropriate actions that are accepted by relevant others." Just because one discovers that appropriate communications have to be authentically based does not mean that one can act on that insight. There is still the question of whether one can perform as well as the insight proscribes. A certain risk is involved here, and the learner has to come through in such a way that relevant others approve of the action and/or saying, which also carries a certain amount of risk. It should be very clear that this type of one-time learning experience is highly intersubjective.

The language of the original description is specific, concrete, and detailed. The psychological description of the same event is more general, condensed, and geared toward the phenomenon being studied—in this case, learning. The psychological description articulates the key meaningful moments and their relationships that are lived in order for learning to take place but not necessarily known as such. The fact that the whole analysis is done within the scientific phenomenological reduction means that the experiencer is responding to the meanings as presented to her without reference as to whether they actually exist as they are presented.

# Chapter 5

# Phenomenology Contra Naturalism: The Need for a Non-Naturalistic Psychological Method

Phenomenology is a distinct philosophy that began at the start of the 20th century (Husserl, 1970). As that century drew to a close, efforts were being made to naturalize phenomenology so that its most distinctive features, its transcendental dimension and its affirmation of irreal objects, would be removed or ignored (Petitot et al., 1999b). I will argue that such an effort is misguided and wrong-headed.

## Philosophical Phenomenology

The philosophy of phenomenology is concerned with consciousness and whatever objects present themselves to consciousness. A phenomenon is anything that appears to consciousness, and phenomenology is concerned with the fact that in the world there are such manifestations as phenomena. It is also concerned with establishing knowledge about such phenomena on a rational, rigorous basis, and so it has scientific ambitions. In its examination of consciousness, phenomenology distinguishes between acts and objects; and among objects it distinguishes between immanent and transcendent ones. The latter objects are external to consciousness, and the former are intrinsic to it.

There is a big difference between how consciousness manifests itself and how transcendent, physical objects do. Transcendent objects, or physical things, are in space, time, and regulated by causality. They are presented adumbrationally, and because of that they are given inadequately. Immanent objects are not physical, and they are given basically as they are—although ultimately also inadequately, for different reasons—and are connected by meaningful relationships.

In order to make essential discoveries about consciousness, Husserlian phenomenologists have adopted a transcendental phenomenological perspective, i.e., a perspective that enables the philosopher to view consciousness in a pure state, purity here indicating that all involvement with empirical or natural reality is severed. This means that the consciousness that is examined is only accessed by means of certain methodical phenomenological procedures and no longer is strictly identifiable by the actually existing type of consciousness that began the analysis. Such a pure consciousness is in no sense naturalistic. From this perspective, phenomenological philosophy is not only non-naturalistic but actually anti-naturalistic. Why then, is an attempt to naturalize consciousness even taking place? Let's look at the arguments.

## The Effort to Naturalize Phenomenology

Since the project is to naturalize phenomenology, we first have to determine what naturalism is. The effort to naturalize phenomenology began primarily, but not exclusively, as a French movement initiated by philosophers and scientists desiring to appropriate phenomenological philosophical insights into a natural scientific framework. The book edited by Petitot, Varela, Pachoud, and Roy (1999a) mentioned above is the primary source wherein the case for naturalizing phenomenology is made, although not all authors agree with this goal and argue against the project. The first chapter provides the primary arguments for attempting to naturalize phenomenology. Subsequent chapters were written by various authors, mostly arguing for and demonstrating how phenomenology has been or could be naturalized. Since the contributors to the various chapters do not necessarily share the same understanding of the meaning of naturalization, my comments will refer to each chapter separately rather than to the book as a whole. I especially find important differences between what the editors of the book (pp. 1–80) say about naturalization and the meaning of naturalization as it is applied by certain authors. I will speak to this difference below, but let's start with the way the naturalization project is articulated by the editors.

According to Roy and colleagues (Roy, Petitot, Pachoud, & Varela 1999, pp. 1–2), "By 'naturalized' we mean integrated into an explanatory framework where every acceptable property is made continuous with the properties admitted by the natural sciences." In other words, all discoveries made by phenomenological investigations have to produce knowledge that is similar to or at least compatible with the results of the natural sciences whose knowledge is based upon investigations of physical phenomena. Thus, the goal of the project to naturalize phenomenology is clear, but the motive is not. Why should knowledge based on the physical sciences be the criterion against which all other knowledge is to be judged? Are all the phenomena of the world physical or reducible to physicalistic expressions? The proponents of naturalization seem to think so because (Petitot et al., 1999b), they write: "Suffice it here to mention the classical computational theory of cognition....whose power of attraction largely rested.... On its seeming ability to offer at long last a viable materialist solution to the mind–body problem — at least as far as cognitive abilities are concerned" (p. xiv). Despite the obvious differences between mental and physical phenomena as they appear in the everyday world, the bias of the cognitive scientists and the proponents of the naturalization of phenomenology is to give a physicalistic account of mental phenomena. It seems as though the mind–body problem can only be resolved by reducing mind to body. These are bold ambitions, so we shall have to see how they hold up. But, first of all, we should look at some features of Husserlian phenomenology to see just how non-naturalistic it is.

### Husserl's Non-Naturalistic Phenomenology

For Husserl (1965, p. 79), "naturalism is a phenomenon consequent upon the discovery of nature, which is to say, nature considered as a unity of spatiotemporal being subject to exact laws of nature." More directly, Chaplin (1968, p. 312) says that naturalism is "the point of view which regards processes as part of the system of natural phenomena and therefore as interpretable according to natural laws." The just-expressed definition makes clear one of Husserl's (1965, p. 80) main objections to naturalism because it results ".... on one hand (in) the naturalizing of consciousness, including all intentionally immanent data of consciousness, and on the other the naturalizing of ideas and consequently of all absolute ideals and norms." For Husserl, consciousness manifests itself differently from nature and cannot be reduced to it. Husserl is as clear as he can be on this point. He writes:

> Psychical being, being as "phenomenon," is in principle not a unity that could be experienced in several separate perceptions as individually identical, not even in perceptions of the same

subject. In the psychical sphere there is, in other words, no distinction between appearance and being .... It is then clear: there is properly speaking, only one nature, the one that appears in the appearance of things. Everything that in the broadest sense of psychology we call a psychical phenomenon when looked at in and for itself, is precisely phenomenon and not nature. A phenomenon, then, is no "substantial" unity; it has no "real properties," it knows no real parts, no real changes, and no causality; all these words are here understood in the sense proper to natural science. (p. 106)

Later Husserl (1965) adds:

The answer, then, is that if phenomena have no nature, they still have an essence, which can be grasped and adequately determined in an immediate seeing.... This, however, is understood as meaning that we remain in the pure phenomenological sphere and leave out of account relationships to nature and to the body experienced as a thing. (p. 110)

Given this account of the incontrovertible distinction between consciousness and the realm of nature, how do the defenders of the effort to naturalize phenomenology propose to accomplish this task? Somehow, they have to account for all of the processes and achievements of consciousness in terms that are naturalistically based, or at least compatible with naturalism. The thinkers who promote the naturalization of phenomenology (e.g., Roy et al., 1999, p. 44) formulate the issues very clearly. They state that there are two key problems to be solved in order to naturalize phenomenology: an epistemological problem and an ontological one. The epistemological problem is whether one can "adequately account for the mental dimension of cognitive phenomena by adopting the explanatory form of questioning and the experimental methodology used in the investigation of natural phenomena." The ontological problem: "Is it possible to transform mental cognitive properties into natural ones?" It is important to acknowledge that these thinkers (Roy et al., 1999, pp. 54–63) base their hope for a naturalization of phenomenology on the scientific motives for Husserl's anti-naturalism. But as Zahavi (2004; 2010) pointed out in his review of this issue, their arguments against scientific phenomenological principles do not touch Husserl's key philosophical tenets.

I think that we should be clear on the nature of the project that the effort to naturalize phenomenology entails. This project is not an integrative one whereby one tries to develop a more comprehensive theory in order to show that apparently antagonistic terms, like mental and physical, can be brought together in a unified theory, which could be a desirable goal. Rather, the project is to convert insights and concepts of one research tradition (the phenomenological one) into an already established alien research tradition that initiated with, and consistently examined, the phenomena of physical nature (Roy et al., 1999, p. 46). The presupposition is that all of the phenomenal manifestations of the world can be comprehended in the same way as the physical phenomena of the world. For some reason there is a rejection of dualistic ontologies despite manifest differences between mental and physical phenomena in the everyday world. Roy et al. (p. 46) write: "The problem (naturalization) can only be answered by making this heterogeneity (between physical and mental) vanish, and thus transforming in one way or another the characterization of the mental properties." The project also runs roughshod over the very idea that the phenomenological research tradition was initiated because it found the pre-existing natural scientific concepts and procedures inadequate for accomplishing the task of comprehending non-physical phenomena.

It is also worth noting that the project very much follows the classical procedures of empirically based natural sciences. All the attempts to prove naturalization follow the basic hypothetic–deductive method of the classical natural sciences. One asserts a hypothesis (all mental phenomena can be explained in terms of the concepts, methods, procedures, etc. of the natural sciences) and then one sets out to prove it by collecting relevant data that purport to support (or not) the hypothesis. Because of the empirical assumptions of this approach, there will always be some sort of sensory data to help support the adjudication of the hypothesis. While there can be questions concerning the empirical basis of a hypothesis, nevertheless, without it the research would not be considered solid. We simply want to note that Husserl's idea of phenomenological science does not function in this manner. His approach is strictly descriptive and is open to non-empirical dimensions of conscious processes (e.g., irreal phenomena such as ideas) as well as empirical givens. Perhaps it was because he understood the difficulty of referring to non-sensorial givens that he invited readers to reflectively follow along with his descriptions and to see if they could confirm what he was describing. In any case, Husserl was well aware of the hypothetical–deductive method but deliberately chose not to follow it in establishing his phenomenological science. Empirically based science was not doing justice to the processes and contributions of consciousness.

The authors (Roy et al., 1999, pp. 46–49) offer diverse arguments for believing in the possibility of the naturalization of phenomenology. I cannot respond to all of the arguments because I do not have a background in all of the disciplines appealed to by the many authors, nor do I have an experiential background in neurological research. I was trained as an experimental psychologist, so I am completely familiar with the natural science perspective. To fit the phenomena of consciousness into that paradigm is indeed a challenge. The authors turn to the history of the natural sciences and claim that something analogous to what they hope to accomplish has already been achieved in the history of natural science, appealing to such historical examples as a basis for hoping that different ontologies can be recategorized. They stress four features that seem to be common when ontological recategorization has historically taken place: (1) the approach of classical mechanics helped bridge the gap between sublunar and supralunar worlds that were thought to be forever incompatible; (2) classical mechanics permitted an abstract level of explanation; (3) the concepts of classical mechanics were able to be transformed into algorithms, and (4) the abstract explanations were able to be integrated with "lower level physical and chemical explanations" (Roy et al., 1999, p. 47).

How well do these examples serve as a model for identifying the differences between the mental and the physical? I'm afraid that the two situations are not so directly comparable. It's understandable that one might, from a naïve perspective, see the sublunar–supralunar distinction as inevitably inviolable. But the critical perspective that science brings to the problem could overcome the alleged dichotomy because the two perspectives are essentially based upon physical givens. But the difference between the mental and the physical as given in the Lifeworld is not along the dimension of physicality. Instead, while one is essentially physical, the other is essentially non-physical. Thus, the gap is essentially qualitatively different from the sublunar–supralunar distinction. Classical mechanics could help resolve the sublunar–supralunar dichotomy because mechanics is the discipline concerned with the motion of physical bodies under the action of forces.

Eventually, it was discovered that whether bodies were sublunar or supralunar did not affect how certain forces influenced them. But what kind of science can straddle the difference between bodies and no bodies (immanent objects like noemata or meanings)? Of course, consciousness only appears in connection with bodies, but such bodies are living beings and not sheer physical entities. It is wrong to reduce the living body to a thing (*Körper*) because where consciousness appears it is always with a biological being pulsating with life (*Leib*). The phenomena of life manifest a type of organization and movement that science does not yet fully understand, and mechanically based movements are analogs of the phenomena of life — i.e., the way in which non-life entities can achieve or approximate or explain the activities that living bodies spontaneously do in other ways. The heart of the issue is how to comprehend the non-sensorial aspects of human beings. Phenomenologically, consciousness and its activities are essential parts contributing to the whole that a human being is. For natural science, consciousness is either epiphenomenal or else can be reduced to some kind of neural (interpreted naturalistically), causal activity.

With respect to the second point, abstract explanations do not disrupt the differences between sublunar and supralunar entities because physicality is the basis of each. But to desire to level the differences between the physical and the mental through abstraction is not precise enough because to satisfy phenomenological criteria what would be required is the abstraction of the essence of the mental. As Husserl (1965, p. 110) said, "… if phenomena have no nature, they still have an essence which can be … determined in an adequate seeing." And if the essence of the mental is radically different from the essence of the physical, what kind of abstraction can straddle such essential differences? It would have to be based on some kind of commonality in the respective modes of being, which is not easily detectable.

The fact that algorithms have now been invented for morphological structures is really neutral with respect to the main issue: the leveling of the differences between the mental and the material. For, as Petitot (1999) says, "The key point is the mathematical schematization of phenomenological descriptive eidetics …. For us, to naturalize an eidetics consists in implementing its mathematical schematization in natural substrates (e.g., neural nets)" (p. 330-331). But, as everyone knows, descriptive eidetics can also remain at the eidetic level (e.g., obtaining the eidos of a logical process). The desire to apply mathematical eidetic schemas to natural processes is what makes the process naturalistic, and the application of the eidetic schemas may even be helpful. But is that making phenomenology naturalistic, or simply using a phenomenological (eidetic) procedure to help clarify a naturalistic process? We believe it is the latter and that it has been done for years, as when statistics or logic has been applied to empirical data.

Finally, with respect to the last point, the authors specify that new knowledge has to be integrated with naturalistic data (physical and chemical explanations). It is the positing of the lower data as naturalistic, with the accompanying demand that the integration be naturalistic, that is problematic. That phenomenology has higher and lower analyses, relationships, and dependencies is evidenced when Husserl speaks about founding–founded relationships. But in such relationships he is not reducing ontological categories. How non-naturalistic procedures can meaningfully relate to naturalistic phenomena would be a real contribution to a difficult problem, but the naturalistic writers rule out that possibility when they insist, a priori, on a naturalistic resolution to each issue.

Thus, the arguments proposed by the authors for recategorizing mental phenomena so that they can be coherently integrated with naturalistic data are not airtight. They present many other arguments as well that may not be as easily dismissed, but their rebuttal requires expertise in many diverse disciplines for which I do not have the necessary background. So, rather than attempt to rebut every argument presented by the authors, I will heed their suggestion (Roy et al., 1999, p. 49) and will examine instead, the work done by Petitot (1999), Varela (1999), and Roy (1999) in order to see how naturalization can be accomplished.

## Ambiguities Concerning the Naturalizing of Phenomenology

In the first chapter, the authors stated what they meant by naturalism: "By 'naturalized' we mean integrated into an explanatory framework where every acceptable property is made continuous with the properties admitted by the natural sciences" (Roy et al., 1999, pp. 1–2). But among those who agree with some type of naturalization project, naturalization is understood differently. Thus, Petit (1999, pp. 241-244), in concluding his argument for naturalization, seems to expand the understanding of naturalization beyond the definition given by the editors.

Petit (1999) reminds the reader that we are always dealing with "living creatures", and as such the body of such creatures is a

"...*Leib,*" "It 'makes sense of', is "oriented toward something (or someone)." Petit then adds: The living being which we are cannot exist without feeling something at some level no matter how "elementary" .... To examine these conditions (mirror neurons, etc.), whether they be ontogenetically acquired or phylogenetically written into the organism, to examine the "living experience of meaning," which may help to explain the meaning giving activity of the subjective and intersubjective being which this organism is, this, it seems to me, opens up a legitimate way of understanding "naturalization." (p. 243)

Well, perhaps, but the "living experience of meaning" is not a theme in the study of nature. Moreover, Petit (1999) wrote, "Phenomenologists should not need to be reminded that this program of naturalization presupposes an intentional and phenomenological psychology, not a behaviorist psychology, still less that of cognitivists who mistakenly suppose that they have moved beyond behaviorism" (p. 244). Is intentionality a part of nature and is phenomenological psychology naturalistic? To me, this sounds more like phenomenologizing science than naturalizing phenomenology. That's another story, and I would certainly be in favor of that. In any case, the sense of naturalization proposed by Petit is at odds with what the editors of the book wrote in the first chapter.

In addition, Varela (1999, p. 267) in his chapter states,

In brief, I approach temporality by following a general research direction I have called *neurophenomenology,* in which lived experience and its natural biological basis are linked by mutual constraints provided by their respective descriptions.... This also means that I will not hesitate when necessary to mix both modes of discourse as if they were partner in a dance, as if they were one, for that is what a naturalized account of phenomena means, and only in action can we see it happening (italics in original).

This may be an advantageous strategy, but to dialogue the language of natural science with phenomenological descriptions is not the same as integrating the latter into an explanatory framework. Varela (1999, p. 267) also states that he will use the phenomenological reduction, which means that he works outside of the natural attitude; but natural science investigations take place within the natural attitude.

What is the principle that guides the interaction of the two attitudes? The meaning of naturalization here is different from the meaning given in the first chapter of the book. One wonders how to ground the "mixing of modes of discourse" when the presuppositions of the two modes of discourse are so different. Yes, they constrain each other, but the "lived body" functions integratedly. How is such integration achieved?

Petitot (1999) ends his chapter on morphological eidetics by stating,

> we hope to have shown that contrary to Husserl's constant claim, there *does* exist a *geometrical* descriptive eidetics able to assume for perception the constitutive tasks of transcendental phenomenology and to mathematize the correlations between the kinetic noetic syntheses and the noematic morphological *Abschattungen.* Using such a geometrical descriptive eidetics, the naturalization of phenomenology can be reduced to the problem of implementing effective algorithms (p. 371; italics in original).

Perhaps this is a solution, but one has to be careful here. One has to be sure that the "effective algorithms" are not merely techniques and that access to intuitions of the phenomena are not missing. On this point, Husserl (1970a) writes:

> Like arithmetic itself (the formal but limited algebraic arithmetic) in technically developing its methodology it is drawn into a process of transformation, through which it becomes a sort of *technique;* that is, it becomes a mere art of achieving, through a calculating technique according to technical rules, results the genuine sense of whose truth can be attained only by concretely intuitive thinking actually directed at the subject matter itself. But now [only] those modes of thought, those types of clarity which are indispensable for a technique as such, are in action. One operates with letters and signs for connections and relations (+, x, =, etc.), according to *rules of the game* for arranging them together in a way essentially not different, in fact, from a game of cards or chess. Here the *original* thinking that genuinely give meaning to this technical process and truth to the correct results (even the

"formal truth" peculiar to the formal *mathesis universalis*) is excluded; in this manner it is also excluded in the formal theory of manifolds itself, as in the previous algebraic theory of number and magnitude and in all the other applications of what has been obtained by a technique, without recourse to the genuine scientific meaning; this includes also the application to geometry, the pure mathematics of spatio-temporal shapes (p. 46, italics in original).

Given the above statement by Husserl, it seems to me that a more extensive argument or a concrete demonstration would be necessary in order to be sure that "effective algorithms" could assume the constitutive tasks of transcendental phenomenology. The mathematics may be correct (I do not have the background to evaluate it) but it seems to me that the justification for the phenomenological claim requires more than simply the application of algorithms.

There are other departures from the definition of naturalization as given by the editors. Barbaras (1999), for example, states that "the naturalization of intentionality makes sense on the condition that Nature be 'de-objectivized', that is, conceived as its own lack, as the unity of itself and life" (p. 538). Smith (1999) puts his finger on the heart of the problem when he states that "Of course everything depends on how naturalism is defined. If intentionality is naturalized in the way of Fodor and Dretske, then I stand with Husserl against 'naturalization.' But if naturalism is defined in the way I shall propose, as unionism in a system of ontological categories, then I accept a 'naturalized' intentionality...." (pp. 84-85). Both Barbaras and Smith highlight the issue of whether intentionality can be naturalized in a way that is consistent with its phenomenological sense and yet can be "integrated into an explanatory framework" consistent with the natural sciences.

I don't want to make a systematic inventory of every chapter to see whether one is in favor of a naturalistically inclined phenomenology or not. The issue will not be resolved by plebiscite. I simply want to show that there were some ambiguities in the very meaning of naturalization, which means that its very achievement is dubious and needs to be interrogated further. Obviously, if the meaning of nature changes, everything has to be started all over again.

## Gallagher's Suggested Strategies for Naturalizing Phenomenology

The phenomenological philosopher Shaun Gallagher (2014, p. 578) is also sympathetic to the naturalization of phenomenology, and he believes that the naturalization project can be accomplished without changing the essence of phenomenology. Gallagher (2014, pp. 578–579) mentions four reasons for being positive about such an attempt. He suggests that one could treat subjective data in an objective way as a means for overcoming their differences; he then suggests that it is possible to make phenomenology explanatory as well as descriptive by using an abstract formal language; a third suggestion is to conceive of phenomenology and cognitive science as mutually constraining, which would involve correlations between neurological data and phenomenological reports; and, finally, Gallagher recommends using a procedure he introduced known as "frontloading phenomenology," which means using distinctions established in phenomenology to influence the design of empirical experiments.

As it turns out, these four strategies really reduce to two. First of all, Gallagher (2014, p. 578) himself rejects the first suggestion and admits that with the first approach one would actually be getting rid of phenomenology. So his first suggestion is not a viable alternative.

The second suggestion recommends using highly abstract phenomenological terms so that formal analyses can be done in conjunction with the usually more abstract terms of the natural sciences. It is interesting to note that with this second approach it is phenomenology that makes all the concessions. Phenomenology does not spontaneously use abstract, third-person formal language to describe its phenomena, and the second approach says that it should. Rather, phenomenology spontaneously uses first-person language and subjective expressions because it finds the articulation of the contents of experiences necessary in order to be faithful to the phenomena as they present themselves. Fidelity to the phenomenon as it is experienced is an inviolable criterion for phenomenology. I suppose that the formalization of phenomenological language could be done (see Marbach, 1993), but does such a procedure help phenomenological analyses or simply make integration with natural sciences easier? If the latter, the question of motive becomes relevant. If following such a procedure means that phenomenological analyses lose their distinctive contributions, how is that a gain for phenomenology? In fact, how is it a gain for science? If phenomenological analyses do make a distinctive contribution to the understanding of phenomena, why would phenomenology want to give up such a contribution so that its integration with formalistic natural science would be easier? Living with the tension between the two approaches may eventually suggest a type of integration whereby neither side loses its strength.

The third suggestion is what is known as the neurophenomenological approach. Here the strategy is to compare phenomenological analyses of persons' experiences with data based on dynamic brain processes. The assumption is that the two sets of data would be mutually constraining or mutually enlightening. Correlating phenomenological descriptions with behavioral or neurological data can certainly be done, but I'm not sure why such procedures should be labelled "naturalistic." The normal body certainly functions in an integrated manner, and tapping into different aspects of that functioning may indeed reveal some interesting findings. But why wouldn't such procedures be seen as a holistic approach or an integrated study rather than a naturalistic one? Why are the so-called naturalistic procedures given priority? Phenomenological analyses are meant to be presuppositionless. Consequently, the analyses would have to be done within an attitude of openness, without priority being assigned to one type of data over the other. The same would be true if behavioral data were being compared to experiential descriptions. Thus, such studies favor naturalism only if naturalistic assumptions are part of the analyses. Operating within the perspective of phenomenological science, one would have to understand discrepancies between data sets in an unbiased way.

Finally, Gallagher (2014, p. 579) suggests using his "frontloading phenomenology" procedure as a way of designing experiments. As Gallagher and Zahavi (2008, p. 38) state it, " The idea is to frontload phenomenological insights into the design of experiments, that is, to allow the insights developed in phenomenological analyses to inform the way experiments are set up." However, once the design incorporating the phenomenological insights has been accomplished, an important part of the results consists of comparing neural processes with experiential data. The difference with neurophenomenology is that "frontloading" specifies more precisely the phenomenological descriptive procedures that are to be implemented, whether subjects are aware of it or not. It should be noted that if phenomenology is "frontloaded" it is often integrated into an empirical research paradigm, and empirical criteria tend to dominate the discussion; as a consequence the power of the phenomenological contribution is truncated because it needs a phenomenological research design in order for its contribution to be made fully manifest.

## Further Reservations Regarding the Naturalization Project

Those who favor the naturalization of phenomenology, even if in a limited sense, point to certain experiments or research strategies as support for their claims. I want to raise some questions about the strategies and/or results of the research conducted for such a purpose. I cannot cover all of the examples in the literature in this chapter, but the article that I will refer to seems to be typical of the reasoning by the promoters of naturalization.

I have chosen Lutz's (2002) article to examine because it was one of the first to initiate the tradition that is being established and encompasses all of the necessary details describing his research. From a phenomenological perspective, I have two questions regarding Lutz's research.

My questions revolve around two primary issues: 1) the real meaning of the confrontation between experiential and neural data, and 2) the description of the experiential phase of the experiment. The neurophenomenologists talk about the confrontation of the two paradigms as fruitful, as a certain advantage that permits mutual enlightenment despite some mutual constraints. I see it as a clash of paradigms whereby it is difficult to interpret findings without prioritizing one of the paradigms. The concepts that rule in one paradigm (meanings, motivational relationships) do not apply in the other (cause–effect relationships, neural processes interpreted mechanically). At times, it seems as though the neural perspective is interpreted as primary since it is seen to be the cause of the experiential. For example, Lutz (2002, p. 133) writes: "In this view, generative passages define the type of circulation which explicitly roots the active and disciplined insight the subject has about his/her experience in a biological emergent process." Later, Lutz (p. 134) adds: "What is at stake is the broadening of the naturalization of experience into the realm of its direct self-manifestation and self-affection. Such a self-referring relation could give immediate insight into the nature of the causal emergent processes that underlie phenomenal appearances." Lutz (p. 146) also writes: "Therefore he/she (observer) cannot provide any direct insight into the nature of the causal process which underlies his/her experience." One might argue that the language here leaves some wiggle room for denying direct causation.

After all, the statements say that the generative passages "root the disciplined insight" and that the causal processes "underlie phenomenal appearances." But if these phrases are interpreted non-causally, how is the "broadening of the naturalization of experience" helped? In this context, experience gets naturalized only if it is shown to be causally dependent upon mechanically interpreted biological processes.

On the other hand, Lutz (2002, p. 139) also writes:

> For instance in this study the two patterns of synchronous oscillations were quite variable in latencies, frequencies, and spatial distribution from repetition to repetition. The source of this variability is believed to reside mainly in fluctuations of the subject's cognitive "context" defined by his attentive state, his spontaneous thought-process, his strategy to carry out the context and so on.

Further on, Lutz (p. 139) adds, "We implement its methodology in the recent study described next, which takes into account first-person data about the cognitive context in order to make understandable a variability in the brain neural responses usually defined as noise." The implication here is that experiential processes can induce or cause neural activity. Lutz (p. 160) thus ends up with a theory of reciprocal causation. A more careful approach would describe the relationship between the experiential processes and the neural data as correlates, which leaves their relationship indeterminate and as a problem to be solved. But the neurophenomenologists are basically thinking within the natural science paradigm, and the phenomenological contribution is equally reduced to its value for naturalistic thinking.

Consequently, I want to stay with the more correct description that the research conducted by the neurophenomenologists represents a clash of paradigms. What is happening is that the phenomenological contribution is being used as an aid for natural scientific thinking, and its full value is not being plumbed. Since the phenomenological contribution to the research is being appropriated by the natural science perspective, it seems as though a type of naturalization is being achieved. However, as a phenomenological psychologist I want to unfold all the implications of the descriptive data and interpret that part of the research in a phenomenologically consistent way. This will show that the two paradigms are not really integrated if one remains faithful to phenomenological standards.

Lutz (2002, pp. 140–143) describes the experimental setting and the procedures that the subjects went through. After extensive training, the subjects were instructed to press a button when they perceived a complete shape on the screen. They were then asked to give a brief verbal report of their experience. Because of the extensive training, we can say that the subjects were knowledgeable about what was to appear. We can also affirm that the subjects were participating in a type of reaction-time experiment that has been conducted by psychologists for over a century. We know from such studies that subjects establish a certain set, or attitude, so that they are ready to respond whenever the appropriate stimulus appears. We also know from the Würzburg studies that the reaction during the experiments is determined primarily by the preparation given to the subjects (Humphrey, 1963, pp. 67–68). Certain "determining tendencies" are established according to the nature of the task. Phenomenologically, we could say that the subjects were experiencing "empty intentions, and, when the full shape appeared, they experienced fulfillment and pressed the button. Of course, the subjects would express their experiences more concretely, but the phenomenological eidetic description holds as well.

Consequently, if the phenomenological aspect of the experiment is given full treatment rather than being foreshortened to merely relate to the neural data, the clash of paradigms continues. Would a neurologist try to argue that he or she has discovered the neural basis for intentionality? But intentionality was taking place all along—while the subjects were being trained, while they waited for the proper stimulus and when the stimulus appeared. Researchers knew that the correct stimulus had appeared because of behavioral data: the button was pressed. Where does the behavioral data fit within the alleged causal chain? Phenomenologically, we would say that the subject, having agreed to participate in the experiment, was motivated to press the button when the stimulus appeared. There was a meaningful relationship among all aspects of the task.

Moreover, the phenomenologist who remains faithful to his or her own research criteria would not participate in conjectures (Lutz, 2002, p. 158), causal analyses (p. 160), or mechanical descriptive terms (p. 137). After all, the body, Leib, is a biological organism, and consciousness always appears where there is life. To understand the emergence of consciousness, we have to understand life better–i.e., non-mechanically. So we have parallel processes going on, experiential and neural, (and we could also add behavioral), although the secret of their relationship is still a puzzle. As Lutz (p. 162) acknowledges in his final sentence, when partial analyses are studied we still have to remember that they are taking place within a well-functioning total organism that is related to a world. Perhaps a genuine holistic perspective is called for rather than simply a dual one that relates only the two variables being manipulated. Perhaps the deciding factor is contributed by the whole organism. Of course, partial studies should be conducted, but they should be interpreted very cautiously.

### Certain Limitations Concerning the Structure and Description of the Experiential Part of Lutz's Experiment

Since I am a phenomenological psychologist, I am quite concerned with the sense of phenomenology that was employed in this experiment because of the ultimate claim that phenomenology can be naturalized. It is my view that such a naturalization is not possible. However, in pursuing that stance, I ran into some practices or orientations that made it difficult for me to come to a definite conclusion. There are two difficulties: 1) pragmatic orientation, and 2) lack of descriptive data. I shall now turn to these issues.

1) **Pragmatic orientation:** Lutz (2002) emphasizes many times that the driving force of his investigation was pragmatic. He writes that, "One of the virtues of Varela's proposition has been to shift this discussion from a strictly abstract and theoretical framework to a pragmatic one that is explicitly anchored in lived experience and open to scientific inquiry" (p. 134). This idea is constantly referred to (pp. 135, 143, 145, 151, 161) and is even considered to be the driving force behind neurophenomenology (p. 136). The question is: What if there is a conflict between pragmatic criteria and phenomenological criteria (or even scientific criteria?) There are indications that pragmatism has won out. Lutz (p. 161) writes that there is the "specific need to start by exploring experience with a rigorous pragmatics before investigating more fully its symbiotic relation to natural entities. .... It is a doable, fruitful and promising approach to the collection of new phenomenal and neurodynamical data and the identification of their mutual relationships." It is not clear what it means to say that "rigorous

dynamics" is guiding the initiation of the study. Also, the assumption that the "collection of new phenomenal and neurodynamical data" (p. 161) will help in the identification of their mutual relationship would not be in line with the phenomenological frame of reference. Now, I want to make clear that I am not in principle against the use of pragmatics in scientific research, especially at the beginning of a tradition. But if pragmatic criteria dominate phenomenological criteria, and then the claim is made that phenomenology has been naturalized, it follows that questions concerning the role of that dominance have to be raised.

2) **Lack of experiential (descriptive) data**: It seems that details concerning the neural phase of the study were more completely presented than those for the experiential phase. For example, Lutz (2002, p. 142) states that "The precise gesture of phenomenological *reduction* was broadly adapted for this study in order to open up the field of investigation" (italics in original). What does it mean to say that the reduction was broadly adapted? Precisely what was changed and how? Husserl gives very explicit instructions concerning the practice of the phenomenological reduction. Perhaps the "broad adaptation" was legitimate, but we need to know precisely what it was. Lutz (p. 142) makes a lot of correct but general statements about the goal of the reduction but the specific instructions to the subjects are not included. Also, Lutz (p. 142) states that the subjects were asked to determine their own invariant phenomenal categories, but no mention is made of the method of free imaginative variation. Finally, the actual descriptions provided by the subjects are not given. Only a couple of examples are given in a footnote (p. 164). It would have been interesting to have a table correlating the specific comments by all subjects with their dynamic neural signatures. It would also have been interesting to see the variability of the neural responses for each trial. Without such data, proper assessment of the results cannot be made.

Even though the exactness of the phenomenological procedures cannot be verified because the specific instructions to the subjects are not given, Lutz (2002, p. 163) claims that his analysis of the experiential data was non-reductive. I will accept that statement, which means that the consciousness of the subjects was in no way naturalized. This also means that a non-naturalized type of consciousness was related to a presumably naturalized process. But is a biological process that belongs to a live body wholly naturalized? Is it perhaps not *Leib* rather than *Körper* that is functioning? And, if so, can we really claim that the process is wholly naturalistic in the sense of the natural sciences? Perhaps the whole relationship has to be rethought since *Leib* partakes of intentionality. If one takes the notion of *Leib* seriously, one should realize that just because there is bodily involvement it does not mean that everything is suddenly naturalistic. One would first have to establish the naturalization of intentionality. From this perspective, "the broadening of the naturalization of experience" (p. 134) becomes questionable.

Consequently, I think that these types of experiments are mislabeled if it is believed that a type of naturalization of consciousness is taking place. Conscious processes are being related to neural processes in a living organism that is being engaged in a task in the world. In such a situation, non-reductive consciousness does not get naturalized; one simply sees one type of concomitant neural brain activity that is correlated with the conscious processes.

I have two remaining questions. The first is that if the conscious processes being described are so brief, I wonder if the use of the reduction is necessary and whether an ordinary, natural attitude description might not be sufficient. My second question is not specific to the experiments but to the whole effort to attempt to naturalize consciousness. I think it is clear that the whole effort depends upon how "nature" is defined. While some of the authors in the Petitot et al. (1999a) book try to define nature differently, those who try to naturalize phenomenology seem to accept the natural science understanding of nature despite Husserl's severe critique of that term. They surely have to be aware that Husserl (1970a, pp. 50–51) wrote "....with Galileo, then, begins the surreptitious substitution of idealized nature for prescientifically intuited nature" and "It is through the garb of ideas that we take for *true being* what is actually a method " (p. 51; italics in original). The idea of nature as posited by natural science is not what is experienced as nature in the Lifeworld. Why then, would phenomenologists want to join the strategies that natural sciences use to study a distorted view of nature?

To their credit, in my reading, the authors arguing for the naturalization of consciousness never try to reduce Husserlian thought in order to try to make it amenable to a naturalistic appropriation. As a matter of fact, they (Roy et al, 1999) acknowledge the greatness of the challenge when they write: "Phenomenology investigates a region of being that is not natural, first, because it is composed of essences of pure lived experiences .... In fact, the whole point of Husserl's enterprise is to claim that there is a dimension of the mental that escapes the natural sciences and requires a specific kind of scientific investigation" (pp. 37-38). Being aware of such Husserlian claims and given their radical nature, why do the authors continue to believe that phenomenology could be naturalized, and for whom would that be helpful? In fact, it is precisely because of such a claim that I think the naturalization of phenomenology project is erroneous and cannot be accomplished. Allow me then to list the reservations and objections that I have to the naturalization project.

## The Idea of Science

A key question that needs to be asked: Is naturalistic science the type of science that Husserl was seeking? The authors (Roy et al., 1999, p. 3) wrote as follows: "More than just a new theory, it (cognitive science) is taken to be the first truly scientific theory of mind ever devised. It is generally considered, for instance, that some mechanism of information processing or dynamical emergence in complex systems have found the appropriate level of explanation, similar to that of forces for motion, or cellular processes for life." But they fail to make explicit that such an idea is a notion of science based precisely on naturalism. But is such a natural scientific expression the type of science that Husserl was seeking?

Husserl (1965, p. 74) has admitted that philosophy is not even off the ground with respect to its scientific status. But he (p. 78) still believed in the possibility of a philosophical science because he wrote that "...the highest interests of human culture demand the development of a rigorously scientific philosophy; (and) it must without fail be animated by the purpose of laying a new foundation for philosophy in the sense of a strict science." Now, naturalism was already in existence when he wrote that statement, and he even admitted that "naturalism sets out with a firm determination to realize the ideal of a rigorously scientific reform of philosophy," adding that with naturalism, "... all this takes place, when we look at it from the standpoint of principle, in a form that from the ground up is replete with erroneous theory" (p. 78). Consequently, how then can cognitive science, which proceeds with naturalistic assumptions and criteria, be the type of science that

Husserl was hoping for? In fact, it was precisely the kind of science he was rejecting.

## For Naturalists, Nature as Part of a Whole Is to Account for the Whole in Terms of Its Own Part Principles

In phenomenology the Lifeworld is the most fundamental given. It is the point of departure for every kind of human or theoretical elaboration — artistic, political, scientific, religious, etc. In the primordially perceived Lifeworld, we find all kinds of events and phenomena, including stones, flowers, storms, earthquakes, mountains, deserts, insects, animals, legal entities, countries, and other humans. The variety is almost endless, but humans have managed to provide categories for the different types of phenomena: physical, biological, human, and for some, spiritual phenomena. With humans, the phenomenon of consciousness presents itself as being radically different from physical phenomena (e.g., it does not present itself through sensory modalities) even though it only appears when associated with living bodies.

The difference between phenomenologists and those who support a naturalistic philosophy is that phenomenologists say that consciousness is irreducible to physical phenomena, whereas the latter want to account for consciousness in terms of categories made to understand physical nature. This motivation is even more puzzling when we remember that nature is determined by subtracting consciousness, or subjectivity, and its phenomena from the original mixed Lifeworld. In other words, world is a totality, and nature is the part of this totality that is constituted by subtracting all conscious or subjective phenomena from the world. The paradox is that from this remnant of the world from which consciousness has been removed — which leaves pure physicality — the naturalists want to account for consciousness and other subjective phenomena. To attempt to understand a whole on the basis of a part is always difficult and usually fails, but to try to understand diverse qualitative phenomena on the basis of a single type seems paradoxical.

It seems that for naturalists the preferred metaphysical presupposition to understand the diversity of the world is monism (phenomenologists are not committed to dualism, but they are committed to understanding all the phenomena of the world according to their essence). It's not that naturalists cannot spontaneously recognize the difference between natural phenomena and other sorts of manifestations but that they will accept qualitatively different types of phenomenal manifestation only if these phenomena can be shown to have evolved from nature as they understand it. Thus, mental events that are thoroughly conscious are easily acceptable as such so long as they can be causally related to complex self-organizing systems that have evolved from nature (emergentism), understood naturalistically. As Petitot et al. (1999b, p. xiv) have written, the goal is "to understand how a *res extensa* could become complex enough through evolution to possess the various attributes of *res cogitans*." For Husserlian phenomenologists, this would mean not only an essential change in how the phenomena manifested themselves but also a transformation of understanding from causal relationships to meaningful implications and motivational relationships. It is not at all clear how such a transformation of principles of understanding could take place while remaining within a naturalistic perspective. It is well known that phenomenologists do not make metaphysical commitments, so they are free to describe phenomena and account for their unfolding and ultimate understanding in whatever terms seem to be called for by the way in which the phenomena present themselves without worrying initially about ultimate explanatory principles.

## The Search for an Authentic Phenomenological Psychology

When Zahavi (2004) reviewed the naturalization of phenomenology project, he allowed that perhaps some type of naturalization could take place with phenomenological psychology because Husserl stated that the transcendental perspective was not necessary when one was functioning as a scientific psychologist because psychological analyses took place within the natural attitude. Husserl sometimes reasoned that the psyche had to be seen as related to nature in such a perspective because of embodiment. However, one has to distinguish between the natural attitude and the naturalistic perspective (and both Husserl and Zahavi do).

It seems to me that Husserl did not work out all the implications of a phenomenological approach within the natural attitude, although he did articulate a detailed understanding of what he had in mind (Husserl, 1977). He certainly would not support a naturalistic type of psychology. But just because psyches appear only in connection with bodies does not mean that a naturalistic perspective is automatically called for. After all, it is because of Husserl's own discovery of the body-subject, or *Leib*, that a reductionistic type of naturalism can be avoided. If intentionality is correlated with consciousness, and the body also partakes of consciousness, and consciousness only appears where there is life, then we have to understand better the relationship between consciousness and life. Why is it that live organisms are oriented towards "other-than-themselves?"

There are levels of directedness toward otherness where there is life that cannot be avoided. These phenomena need to be studied and understood much better than they are. They call for an extension of consciousness downward rather than an extension of physicality upwards. In any case, it seems to me that such thinking provides a basis for a non-naturalistic but world-related psychology, and it is Husserl himself who has provided such a perspective. If we think of the natural attitude as encompassing subjectivity, as "being-in-the-world" rather than as being based on a distorted understanding of nature, then the basis for a non-naturalistic phenomenological psychology is established. While the notion of "being-in-the-world" is popularly related to Heidegger, it is also in Husserl, and it is what motivates the transcendental reduction. To move from psychology to philosophy is to move from world-relatedness (or intertwinement of subjectivity and world) to world constituting. This understanding breaks all ties with a naturalistic psychology because being world-related is not the same as being dependent on nature, especially as natural science defines it. It would be a phenomenological psychology within the natural attitude but non-naturalistically understood.

## Gurwitsch's Views on Psychology

I will approach the search for an authentic phenomenological psychology on the basis of an article that Gurwitsch (1934, 1966) wrote some time ago. All the ideas Gurwitsch expresses are similar to those of Husserl, but Gurwitsch (1966) in this article focuses on the very meaning of psychology in an enlightening way. Gurwitsch, raises the question of the place of psychology in the system of the sciences and relates the problem of psychology's standing to the fact that psychology and physics were born more or less at the same time, and the superior development of the natural sciences led to psychology's adoption "of the methods and principles of physics" (Gurwitsch, 1966, p. 57). He (pp. 56–64) traces the development of psychology not by starting with Wundt, as modern psychologists do, but back to the 17th and 18th centuries and says that "The thinkers who witnessed the birth of the mathematical and physical sciences, such as Descartes, Hobbes, Locke, Condillac, and Berkeley, were the originators of modern psychology."

He also follows Cassirer in stating that Malebranche developed the first system of scientific psychology as we would understand it today. One consequence of this historical fact is that psychology tried to imitate physics, and during its history, psychology "more than once (has) been conceived as a kind of 'physics of the soul'" (Gurwitsch, 1966, p. 57).

Gurwitsch then goes on to show that such a conception could only lead to a very limited contribution to knowledge by psychology. If physics was the ideal science, then psychology had to remain as close as possible to physics and its ideals. Gurwitsch (p. 57) wisely states: "The main reason for the restricted nature of psychological studies, even when enlarged to their ultimate limits, is that they depend upon biological and, in particular, physiological research, in such a way that the universal laws of physics and chemistry intervene and support the work of the psychologist from the very outset." Consequently, the major achievement for psychology from this perspective would be to establish "within its own realm laws analogous to physics or chemistry" (p. 58). Gurwitsch then articulates what can be called a naturalistic desire or ambition for psychology. He writes:

> Such success would constitute for psychology the proof of its scientific character, for the realm of consciousness would be integrated into the whole of the universe: the same laws that govern nature would be shown to equally govern consciousness which would thereby truly appear as one of its domains. The scientific conquest of the world would be extended to one more region. (p. 58)

Is this desire the driving force behind the naturalization of phenomenology? Of course, it is understandable that at the lower levels of life, with sympathetic interpretations, the methods of the natural sciences can still be relatively effective. But such procedures reach a breaking point at higher levels of life, and other modes of thinking are called for. As long as natural science is the framework within which one thinks, no genuine breakthroughs can happen. We see that this attitude prevails even today since in Lutz's (2002) study neurology as a natural science was conceived to be the cause, or the effect, of certain experiential processes. That is, neurology is conceived of as being a natural science even though the research deals with an aspect of a live human organism that is engaged with a task in the world. In any event, Gurwitsch (1966) then goes through the major schools of psychology from associationistic psychology, through Herbart, psychoanalysis, and

Gestalt theory to show how the thinking of the psychological schools is analogous to the thinking in physics.

Instead, psychology's basis has to be different from that of the physical sciences. Gurwitsch (1966, p. 64) wrote

> that the decisive difference between psychology and the sciences of physics and chemistry consists in that it is precisely the very "subjective" data and qualities discarded by these sciences which constitute the subject matter of psychology.... Of equal .... Importance is the very fact that the ambient world in which we live carries the imprint of humanity: it is a human world.

Gurwitsch is basically saying what Husserl advised: We must go back to the Lifeworld to found our science. If we are interested in founding a science that will do justice to human consciousness, then we have to base that science on how consciousness manifests itself in the world. We need a science that supports an attitude that is harmonious with the human attitude displayed in the everyday world. Gurwitsch never forgets the role of human consciousness in establishing science. He (1966, p. 64) notes an important discrepancy in that the human world has significance and relevancy for us as opposed to the world of natural science, which takes its departure from "neutral objects .... that are constructed by science, that is to say, by the scientific endeavors of the human mind." He is intrigued by the general way of looking at things through the attitude of natural science, adding that that within science:

> There are methods and procedures which are alien to the natural naïveté of man but indispensable to scientific constructions. To mention only one problem: abstracting from the qualities of instrumentality, of value, and also from secondary qualities, seeing in every object only a special case of a physical body in general to which the laws of physics apply, requires a mental operation in whose nature, conditions, presuppositions and origin psychology cannot help being interested. (p. 66)

It seems to me that Gurwitsch has articulated quite well the reason that the project to naturalize phenomenology is problematic. Phenomenology, with its comprehensive perspective, finds itself dealing with subjectivity and its processes because the physical sciences choose to deal with only physical phenomena or phenomena from which subjective presences have been removed. Thus, when a physicist encounters a mixed "subjective–physical" phenomenon, he abstracts the subjective, and the discipline becomes the study of a physical phenomenon. When phenomenology deals with purely physical phenomena, it does so within the "consciousness of physical phenomena." Or better yet, it is the study of "the consciousness of the consciousness of physicality." It is a reflective enterprise. The role of the consciousness of the researcher is always included because it is constitutive of the very objects of science.

There are more implications, so let's continue with what Gurwitsch (1966) says:

> In this world of everyday experience we can see a sort of natural illusion, an error into which our human constitution forces us and from which science emancipates us without, however, making the illusion disappear altogether .... The true structure of reality may be as science reveals it. However, not only must scientific theories be verified in terms of subjective" phenomena and our experiences of them, but, what is more, it is only by starting from the ambient world in which we never cease to exist that the scientific conquest of reality can be undertaken. (pp 65–66)

The import of Gurwitsch's views, which in this case are harmonious to those of Husserl, is that the initial situation is one of subjectivity intermingled with physical nature, which could be called "phenomenologized nature," and it is precisely that mixture that has to be understood. Once nature is separated from consciousness no amount of extension or transformation of naturalistic concepts or procedures can enable them to analyze conscious or subjective phenomena adequately. Because of the way that conscious phenomena manifest themselves, they require a different set of concepts and different principles of understanding.

Finally, Gurwitsch (1966, p. 68) reminds us that "Consciousness is the general medium of constitution. Every objective universe, the ambient world of everyday life as well as the scientific representation of the world, arises through acts of consciousness." Given the above phenomenological understanding of consciousness, Gurwitsch is able to assign a place for psychology among the system of sciences. He says:

[Psychology's] main task is not to enrich our knowledge of reality as the physical and chemical sciences do but to account for the very knowledge of reality. In this manner psychology approaches philosophy, which is to say that by a sufficient radicalization of the problems of psychology we reach the philosophical dimension. (p. 68)

If it is part of psychology's task to understand how knowledge is won, then it is even more critical that we understand well the type of science psychology is, if only to know how to evaluate our knowledge claims. Because the role of consciousness is absolutely central for psychology, and since from a phenomenological perspective the transcendental attitude is essential for understanding consciousness, then it would seem that the transcendental perspective would have to be involved in some way in establishing how we understand psychological consciousness. In any case, the line of thinking established by Husserl and Gurwitsch solidly establishes a basis for a non-naturalistic psychology, and the clear implication is that we need a non-naturalistic method. Husserl, of course, has already provided us with a philosophical, non-naturalistic method and with suggestions as to how a phenomenological psychological method might be practiced, but the latter is more dubious than the former. I, (Giorgi, 2009) have worked out one way that a phenomenological psychological method might be practiced, but I am not at all confident that the last word concerning how a phenomenological psychological method might be practiced has been written.

Of course, there are publications (Zahavi, 2004, 2010; Moran, 2008) showing philosophically how difficult it would be for phenomenology to be naturalized. But I have tried here to show that even scientifically the naturalization of phenomenology is not desirable. That is why I concentrated on Gurwitsch's views on psychological science, which indicate that the very phenomena to be understood psychologically transcend the naturalistic viewpoint. It leads to the deeper question of whether one can conceive of a transcendental science and of how it might be practiced differently from philosophical phenomenology. I know that philosophers claim that the transcendental perspective is peculiarly philosophical, but if at a deep level transcendentality cannot be removed from consciousness without distorting its essence, it may be that sciences dealing with conscious phenomena may also have to include it.

In any case, the major implication of the above analyses is that science has to be phenomenologized rather than that phenomenology be naturalized. I have been told that Varela had this in mind as well, although it seems that he did not get around to implementing this task as much as the naturalization project.

# References

Addison, R.B. (1989). Grounded interpreted research: An investigation of physician socialization. In M.J. Packer & R.B. Addison (Eds.), *Entering the circle: Hermeneutic investigation in psychology*. Albany, NY: State University of New York Press.

Barbaras, R. (1999). The movement of the living as the originary foundation of intentional movement. In J. Petitot, F.J. Varela, B. Pachoud, & J-M Roy (Eds.), *Naturalizing phenomenology* (pp. 525–538). Stanford, CA: Stanford University Press.

Betti, E. (1955). *Teoria generale della interpretazione*. Milan: Dott. A. Giuffrè.

Blumer, H. (1969). *Symbolic interactionism*. Englewood Cliffs, NJ: Prentice-Hall, Inc.

Bohman, J.F. (1991). Holism without skepticism: Contextualism and the limits of interpretation. In D.R. Hiley, J.F. Bohman, & R. Shusterman (Eds.), *The interpretive turn* (pp. 129–154). Ithaca, NY: Cornell University Press.

Brentano, F. (1973). *Psychology from an empirical standpoint* (O. Kraus & L. McAlister, Eds.; A Rancurello, D. B. Terrell, & L. L. McAlister, Trans.). New York, NY: Humanities Press. (Original work published in 1874)

Brown, L.M., Tappan, M.B., Gilligan, C., Miller, B.A., & Argyris, D.E. (1989). Reading for self and moral voice. A method for interpreting narratives of real-life moral conflict and choice. In M.J. Packer & R.B. Addison (Eds.), *Entering the circle: Hermeneutic investigation in psychology* (pp. 141–164). Albany, NY: State University of New York Press.

Bruzina, R. (2004). *Edmund Husserl & Eugen Fink*. New Haven, CT: Yale University Press.

Buchler, J. (1940). *The philosophy of Peirce: Selected writings*. London: Routledge & Kegan Paul.

Chaplin, J. P. (1968). *Dictionary of psychology*. New York, NY: Dell Publishing Co.

Charmaz, K. (2000). Grounded theory: Objectivist and constructivist methods. In N.K. Denzin & Y.S. Lincoln (Eds.), *Handbook of qualitative research* (2nd ed.; pp. 509–535) London: Sage Publications.

Charmaz, K. (2006). *Constructing grounded theory*. London: Sage Publications.

Charmaz, K. (2014). *Constructing grounded theory* (2nd ed.). London: Sage Publications.

Clarke, A. E. (2005). *Situational analysis.* London: Sage Publications.

Corbin, J., & Strauss, A. (2008). *Basics of qualitative research.* London: Sage Publications.

Denzin, N.K. (1994). The art and politics of interpretation. In N.K. Denzin & Y. S. Lincoln (Eds.), *Handbook of qualitative research* (pp. 500–515). London: Sage Publications.

Denzin, N.K. & Lincoln, Y.S. (Eds.). (2000). *Handbook of qualitative research* (2nd ed.). London: Sage Publications.

Dewey, J. (1973). The development of American pragmatism. In J. J. McDermott (Ed.), *The philosophy of John Dewey* (Vol. 1; pp. 41–58). New York, NY: G.P. Putnam's Sons. (Original work published in 1925)

Dewey, J. (1998a). The postulate of immediate empiricism. In L.A. Hickman & T.M. Alexander (Eds.), *The essential Dewey* (pp. 115–120). Bloomington IN: Indiana University Press. (Original work published in 1905)

Dewey, J. (1998b). The need for a recovery of philosophy. In L.A. Hickman & T.M. Alexander (Eds.), *The essential Dewey* (pp. 46–70). Bloomington IN: Indiana University Press. (Origin work published in 1917)

Dilthey, W. (1977). A descriptive and analytic psychology. In R. M. Zaner & K.L. Heiges (Eds.), *Descriptive psychology and historical understanding* (pp. 21–120; R.M. Zaner, Trans.). Germany: Martinus Nijhoff. (Original work published in 1894)

Douglass, B., & Moustakas, C. (1985). Heuristic inquiry: The internal search to know. *Journal of Humanistic Psychology, 25,* 39–55.

Freud, S. (1900). The interpretation of dreams. In A.A. Brill (Ed. & Trans.), *The basic writings of Sigmund Freud* (pp. 181–549). New York, NY: The Modern Library.

Gadamer, H-G. (1975). *Truth and method.* (G. Barden & J. Cumming, Trans.). London: Sheed and Ward. (Original work published in 1960)

Gadamer, H-G. (1979). The problem of historical consciousness. In P. Rabinow & W.M. Sullivan (Eds.), *Interpretive social science: A second look* (pp. 82–140). Berkeley, CA: University of California Press.

Gallagher, S. (2014) Cognitive science. In Luft, S. & Overgaard, S. (Eds.), *The Routledge companion to phenomenology.* London: Routledge.

Gallagher, S. & Zahavi, D. (2008) *The phenomenological mind.* London. Routledge.

Gallagher, S. & Zahavi, D. (2012). *The phenomenological mind* (2nd ed.). New York, NY: Routledge.

Giorgi, A. (1975). An application of the phenomenological method in psychology. In A. Giorgi, C. Fischer, & E.L. Murray (Eds.), *Duquesne studies in phenomenological psychology* (Vol. II; pp. 82–103). Pittsburgh, PA: Duquesne University Press.

Giorgi, A. (1985). The phenomenological psychology of learning and the verbal learning tradition. In A. Giorgi (Ed.), *Phenomenology and psychological research* (pp. 23–85). Pittsburgh, PA: Duquesne University Press.

Giorgi, A. (1986). The "Context of discovery/Context of verification" distinction and descriptive human science. *Journal of Phenomenological Psychology, 17,* 5–20.

Giorgi, A. (2009). *The descriptive phenomenological method in psychology: A modified Husserlian approach.* Pittsburgh, PA: Duquesne University Press.

Giorgi, A. (2014). An affirmation of the phenomenological psychological descriptive method: A response to Rennie (2012). *Psychological Methods, 19,* 542–551.

Glaser, B. (1978). *Theoretical sensitivity.* Mill Valley, CA: Sociology Press.

Glaser, B. (1992). *Basics of grounded theory analysis.* Mill Valley, CA: Sociology Press.

Glaser, B. (2003). *The grounded theory perspective.* Mill Valley, CA: Sociology Press.

Glaser B. & Strauss, A. (1967). *The discovery of grounded theory: Strategies for qualitative research.* Chicago, IL: Aldine Publishing Co.

Gurwitsch, A. (1934). La place de psychologie dans la systeme de sciences. *Revue de Synthese,* Vol. viii.

Gurwitsch, A. (1966). Studies in phenomenology and psychology. In *The collected works of Aron Gurwitsch* (1901–1903; Vol. II). Evanston, IL: Northwestern University Press.

Gurwitsch, A. (1973). Perceptual coherence as the foundation of the judgment of predication. In F. Kersten and R. Zaner (Eds.), *Phenomenology: Continuation and criticism. Essays in memory of Dorion Cairns* (pp. 62–89). The Hague: Martinus Nijhoff.

Heidegger, M. (1962). *Being and time* (J. Macquarrie & E. Robinson, Trans.). New York, NY: Harper & Row. (German original published 1927).

Hirsch, E.D. Jr. (1967). *Validity in interpretation*. New Haven, CT: Yale University Press

Humphrey, G. (1963) *Thinking: An introduction to its experimental psychology*. New York, NY: John Wiley & Sons.

Husserl, E. (1960). Cartesian meditations (D. Cairns, Trans.). The Hague: Martinus Nijhoff. (Original work published in 1929)

Husserl, E. (1965). Philosophy as a rigorous science. In Q. Lauer (Ed.), *Phenomenology and the crisis of philosophy* (pp. 71–148). New York, NY: Harper Torchbooks. (German original published in 1911)

Husserl, E. (1970a). *Logical investigations* (J.N. Findlay, Trans.). New York, NY: Humanities Press. (Original work published in 1900)

Husserl, E. (1970b). *The crisis of European sciences and transcendental phenomenology* (D. Carr, Trans.). Evanston, IL: Northwestern University Press. (Original work published in 1954)

Husserl, E. (1973). *Experience and judgment* (J.S. Churchill & K. Ameriks, Trans.). Evanston, IL: Northwestern University Press. (Original work published in 1948)

Husserl, E. (1977). *Phenomenological psychology* (J. Scanlon, Trans.). The Hague: Martinus Nijhoff (Original work published in 1962)

Husserl, E. (1978). *Formal and transcendental logic* (D. Cairns, Trans.). The Hague: Martinus Nijhoff. (Original work published in 1974)

Husserl, E. (1983). *Ideas pertaining to a pure phenomenology and to a phenomenological philosophy*. First Book (F. Kersten, Trans.). The Hague: Martinus Nijhoff. (Original work published in 1913)

Husserl, E. (1997). Appendix Three: Phenomenology and anthropology. In T. Sheehan & R.E. Palmer (Eds. & Trans.), *Edmund Husserl: Psychological and transcendental phenomenology and the confrontation with Heidegger* (1927–1931; pp. 485–500). Dordrecht: Kluwer Academic Publishers. (German original: Lecture delivered in 1931).

Husserl, E. (2006). *The basic problems of phenomenology* (I. Farin & J.G. Hart, Trans.). Dordrecht, Holland: Springer. (Original work published in 1973)

James, W. (1907). *Pragmatism: A new name for an old way of thinking.* New York, NY: Longmans, Green & Co.

Keen, E. (1975). *Doing psychology phenomenologically: Methodological considerations.* Unpublished Manuscript. Bucknell University.

Lutz, A. (2002). Toward a neurophenomenology as an account of generative passages: A first empirical case study. *Phenomenology and the Cognitive Sciences, 1,* 133–167.

Marbach, E. (1993). *Mental representation and consciousness: Towards a phenomenological theory of representation and reference.* Dordrecht: Kluwer.

Merleau-Ponty, M. (1962). *The phenomenology of perception* (C. Smith, Trans.). New York, NY: Humanities Press. (Original work published in 1945)

Miller, D.L. (1973). *George Herbert Mead: Self, language and the world.* Austin, TX: University of Texas Press.

Mohanty, J.N. (1972) *The concept of intentionality.* St. Louis, MO: Warren H. Green Inc.

Mohanty, J.N. (1987). Philosophical description and descriptive philosophy. In *Phenomenology: Descriptive or hermeneutic* (pp. 39–61). Pittsburgh PA: Simon Silverman Phenomenology Center, Duquesne University.

Moneta, G. (1972). The foundation of predicative experience and the spontaneity of consciousness. In L. Embree (Ed.), *Life-world and consciousness: Essays for Aron Gurwitsch* (pp. 171–190). Evanston, IL: Northwestern University Press.

Moran, D. (2008). Husserl's transcendental philosophy and the critique of naturalism. *Continental Philosophical Review, 41,* 401–425.

Moustakas, C. (1961). *Loneliness.* Englewood Cliffs, NJ: Prentice-Hall.

Moustakas, C. (1967). *Heuristic research.* In J.F.T. Bugental (Ed.), *Challenges of humanistic psychology* (pp. 101–107). New York, NY: McGraw-Hill.

Moustakas, C. (1968). *Individuality and encounter.* Cambridge MA: Howard A. Doyle Pub. Co.

Moustakas, C. (1972). *Loneliness and love.* Englewood Cliffs, NJ: Prentice-Hall Inc.

Moustakas, C. (1975). *The touch of loneliness.* Englewood Cliffs, NJ: Prentice-Hall Inc.

Moustakas, C. (1988). *Phenomenology, science and psychotherapy.* Sydney, Nova Scotia: Family Life Institute, University College of Cape Breton.

Moustakas, C. (1990). *Heuristic research*. Newbury Park, CA: Sage Publications.

Moustakas, C. (1994). *Phenomenological research methods*. Thousand Oaks, CA: Sage Publications.

Packer, M.J. (1989). Tracing the hermeneutic circle: Articulating an ontical study of moral conflicts. In M.J. Packer & R.B. Addison (Eds.), *Entering the circle: Hermeneutic investigation in psychology* (pp. 95–118). Albany, NY: State University of New York Press.

Packer, M.J. (2011). *The science of qualitative research*. Cambridge: Cambridge University Press.

Packer, M.J. & Addison, R.B. (Eds.). (1989). *Entering the circle: Hermeneutic investigation in psychology*. Albany, NY: State University of New York Press.

Packer, M.J. & Addison, R.B. (1989a). Evaluating an interpretive account. In M.J. Packer & R.B. Addison (Eds.), *Entering the circle: Hermeneutic investigation in psychology* (pp. 275–292). Albany, NY: State University of New York Press.

Packer, M.J. & Addison, R.B. (1989b). Introduction. In M.J. Packer & R.B. Addison (Eds.), *Entering the circle: Hermeneutic investigation in psychology* (pp. 13–38). Albany, NY: State University of New York Press.

Palmer, R.E. (1969). *Hermeneutics*. Evanston, IL: Northwestern University Press.

Peirce, C.S. (1986). How to make our ideas clear. In J.W. Kloesel (Ed.), *Writings of Charles S. Peirce: A chronological edition* (Vol. 3, pp. 257–276). Bloomington, IN: Indiana University Press. (Original work published in 1878)

Petit, J-L. (1999) Constitution by movement: Husserl in light of recent neurobiological findings. In Petitot, J., Varela, F.J., Pachoud, B., & Roy, J-M. (Eds.) *Naturalizing phenomenology* (pp. 220–244). Stanford, CA: Stanford University Press.

Petitot, J. (1999) Morphological eidetics for a phenomenology of perception. In Petitot, J., Varela, F.J., Pachoud, B., & Roy, J-M. (Eds.) *Naturalizing phenomenology* (pp. 330–371). Stanford, CA. Stanford: University Press.

Petitot, J., Varela, F.J., Pachoud, B., & Roy, J-M. (Eds.) (1999a). *Naturalizing phenomenology*. Stanford, CA: Stanford University Press.

Petitot, J., Varela, F.J., Pachoud, B., & Roy, J-M. (Eds.) (1999b). Foreword. In Petitot, J., Varela, F.J., Pachoud, B., & Roy, J-M.

(Eds.), *Naturalizing phenomenology* (pp. xiii–xvi). Stanford, CA: Stanford University Press.

Piaget, J. (1932). *The moral judgment of the child*. London: Kegan Paul.

Politzer, G. (1968). *Critiques des fondemonts de la psychologie*. Paris: Presses Universitaires de France. (Original work published in 1928)

Rabinow, P., & Sullivan, W.M. (1987). The interpretive turn: A second Look. In P. Rabinow & W.M. Sullivan (Eds.), *Interpretive social science: A second look* (pp. 1–30). Berkeley, CA: University of California Press.

Radnitsky, G. (1970). *Contemporary schools of metascience*. Göteborg, Sweden: Akademiförlaget.

Reck, A.J. (Ed.). (1964). *Selected writings: George Herbert Mead*. New York, NY: The Bobbs-Merrill Company.

Rennie, D. (2012). Qualitative research as methodical hermeneutics. *Psychological Methods, 17,* 385–398.

Ricoeur, P. (1981). *Paul Ricoeur: Hermeneutics and the human sciences* (J.B. Thompson, Ed. & Trans.). Cambridge: Cambridge University Press. (Original work published in 1975)

Ricoeur, P. (1981a). The task of hermeneutics. In J.B. Thompson (Ed. & Trans.), *Paul Ricoeur: Hermeneutics and the human sciences* (pp. 43–62). Cambridge: Cambridge University Press.

Ricoeur, P. (1981b). The model of a text: Meaningful action considered as a text. In J.B. Thompson (Ed. & Trans.), *Paul Ricoeur: Hermeneutics and the human sciences* (pp. 197–221). Cambridge: Cambridge University Press.

Ricoeur, P. (1981c). Phenomenology and hermeneutics. In J.B. Thompson (Ed. & Trans.), *Paul Ricoeur: Hermeneutics and the human sciences* (pp. 101–128). Cambridge: Cambridge University Press.

Rosensohn, W.L. (1974). *The phenomenology of Charles S. Peirce*. Amsterdam: Grüner B.V.

Roy, J-M. (1999). Saving intentional phenomena: Intentionality, representation symbol. In J. Petitot, F.J. Varela, B. Pachoud, & J-M Roy (Eds), *Naturalizing phenomenology* (pp. 111-147) Stanford, CA: Stanford University Press.

Roy, J-M., Petitot, J., Pachoud, B., & Varela, F.J. (1999). Beyond the gap: An introduction to naturalizing phenomenology. In Petitot, J., Varela, F.J., Pachoud, B., & Roy, J-M (Eds.), *Naturalizing phenomenology* (pp.1–80). Stanford, CA: Stanford University Press.

Schmitt, R. (1968). Husserl's transcendental-phenomenological reduction. In J.J. Kockelmans (Ed.), *Phenomenology* (pp. 58–68). Garden City, NY: Doubleday.

Shusterman, R. (1991). Beneath interpretation. In D.R. Hiley, J.F. Bohman & R. Shusterman (Eds.), *The interpretive turn* (pp. 102–128). Ithaca, NY: Cornell University Press.

Simon, H. & Ericsson, K.A. (1980). Verbal reports as data. *Psychological Review, 87*, 215–251.

Smith, B. (1999) Truth and the visual field. In J. Petitot, F.J. Varela, B. Pachoud, & J-M Roy (Eds.), *Naturalizing phenomenology* (pp. 317–329). Stanford, CA: Stanford University Press.

Speake, J. (Ed.) (1979). *A dictionary of philosophy*. London: Pan Books.

Spence, D.P. (1989). Rhetoric vs. evidence as a source of persuasion: A critique of the case study genre. In M.J. Packer & R.B. Addison (Eds.), *Entering the circle: Hermeneutic investigation in psychology* (pp. 205–222). Albany, NY: State University of New York Press.

Strauss, A. (1987). *Qualitative analysis for social scientists*. Cambridge: Cambridge University Press.

Taylor, C. (1985). Interpretation and the sciences of man. In C. Taylor (Ed.), *Philosophy and the human sciences: Philosophical papers 2* (pp. 15–57). Cambridge: Cambridge University Press.

Titchener, E.B. (1901a). *Experimental psychology: A manual of laboratory practice* (Vol. 1, Qualitative experiments, part 1, Student's manual). New York, NY: Macmillan.

Titchener, E.B. (1901b). *Experimental psychology: A manual of laboratory practice* (Vol. 1, Qualitative experiments, part 2, Instructor's manual). New York, NY: Macmillan.

Varela, F.J. (1999) The specious present: A neurophenomenology of time consciousness. In Petitot, J., Varela, F.J., Pachoud, B., & Roy, J-M. (Eds.) *Naturalizing phenomenology* (pp. 266–314). Stanford, CA: Stanford University Press.

van Kaam, A. (1966). *Existential foundations of psychology*. Pittsburgh PA: Duquesne University Press.

Wertz, F., Charmaz, K., McMullen, L.M., Josselson, R., Anderson R., & McSpadden, E. (2011). *Five ways of doing qualitative analysis*. New York, NY: The Guilford Press.

Zahavi, D. (2004). Phenomenology and the project of naturalization. *Phenomenology and the Cognitive Sciences, 3*, 331–347.

Zahavi, D. (2010). Naturalized phenomenology. In S. Gallagher & D. Schmicking (Eds.), *Handbook of phenomenology and cognitive science* (pp. 3–19). Dordrecht: Springer Science.

Zaner, R. (1972). Reflections on evidence and criticism in the theory of consciousness. In L. Embree (Ed.), *Life-world and consciousness: Essays for Aron Gurwitsch* (pp. 209–230). Evanston, IL: Northwestern University Press.

# Author Biography

Amedeo Giorgi received his PhD in psychology from Fordham University in 1958 and first taught at Manhattan College and then at Duquesne University. He was trained in experimental psychology and he pursued a career in academic psychology. He found the standard experimental and quantitative procedures being pursued by mainstream psychology to be too limited for human phenomena so he turned to phenomenological philosophy as the basis for a non-reductionistic and non-naturalistic philosophical anthropology. He is the author of *Psychology as a Human Science* and *The Descriptive Phenomenological Method in Psychology*, and was the founder of the *Journal of Phenomenological Psychology* and its first editor for 25 years. He transferred to Saybrook University in 1986 where he taught courses in phenomenological methodology and phenomenological psychology. From 1990 until 1995 he held a joint appointment with the francophone University of Quebec at Montreal (UQAM). He is currently Professor Emeritus at Saybrook and continues to write articles demonstrating the value of phenomenological approaches to psychological phenomena.